On Fragile Wings

ROSE HOLLAND BROWN

On Fragile Wings

ISBN: 978-1-60414-554-0

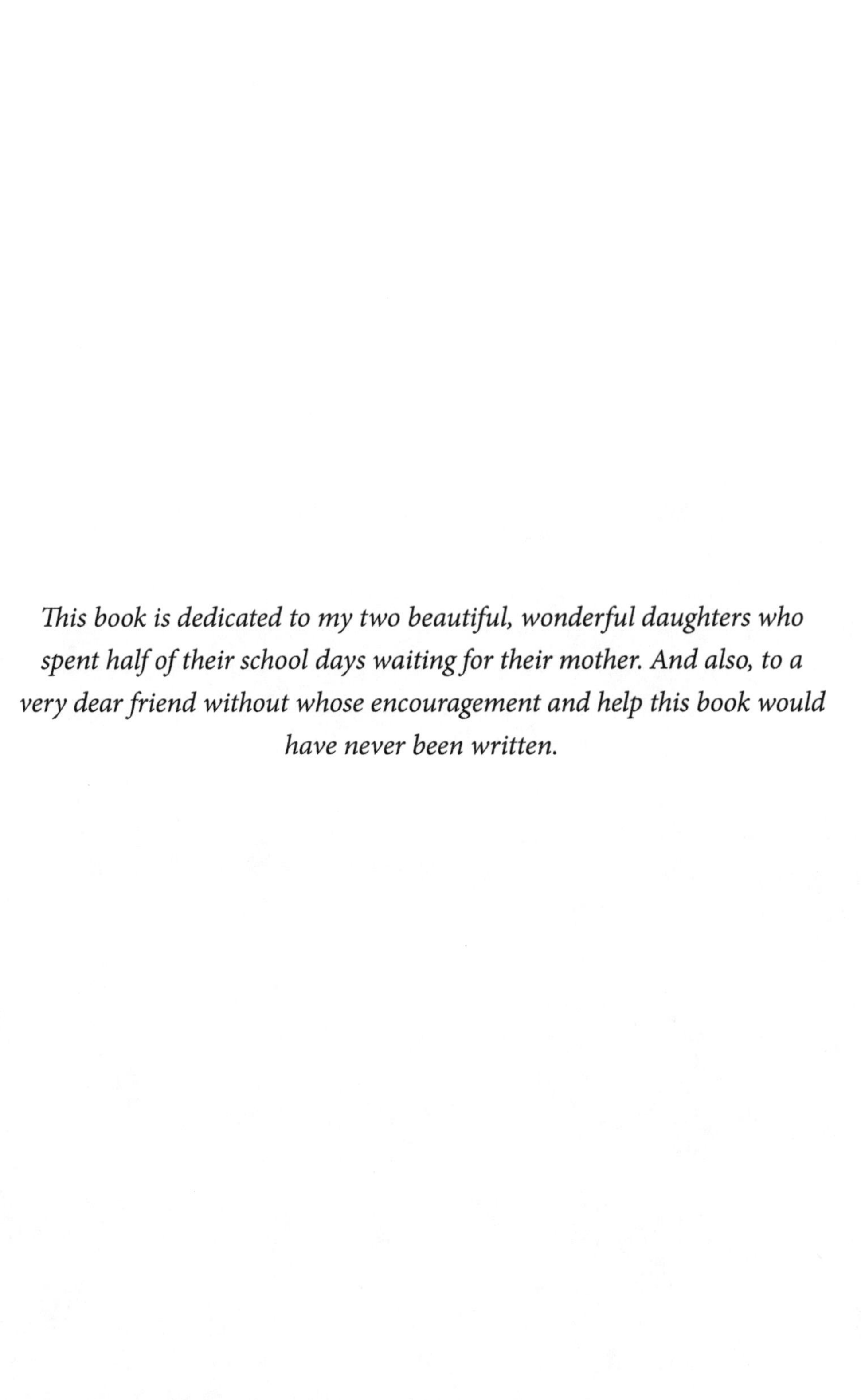

This book is dedicated to my two beautiful, wonderful daughters who spent half of their school days waiting for their mother. And also, to a very dear friend without whose encouragement and help this book would have never been written.

Table of Contents

CHAPTER 5

CHAPTER 6

CHAPTER 7

CHAPTER 8

CHAPTER 9

CHAPTER 10

CHAPTER 11

CHAPTER 12

CHAPTER 13

CHAPTER 14

CHAPTER 15

CHAPTER 16

CHAPTER 17

CHAPTER 18

CHAPTER 19

CHAPTER 1

Introduction

"If you plan to stay in this school, you had better clean up your act, cut your hair and say 'Yes, sir' and 'Yes, ma'am' when you are spoken to. Is that clear?" Raz bellowed this out to all of the students in the gym.

However, I am getting ahead of myself. This is an introduction! I need to lead you into this gently, very gently, because some of this makes some tough reading.

When I thought about writing an introduction to this book, I hardly knew how to start. Nevertheless, I felt that I owed the reader a little of my background and I also needed to explain the reasons that I felt so compelled to write about my wonderful students. I never intended to make this book an invasion of their privacy. That privacy means a lot to me and I want to guard it. Most of the names are changed. All else is real, too real for words. This book is intended to give insight into some of the difficulties that young people have in becoming adults and overcoming the many stumbling blocks that are placed in their way. I intended it to help other young people who pass the same way, those who pass along the same path to adulthood. I intended it to help adults who work with young people to urge them to tread gently, to listen well, and to ask the right questions.

I also intended it for parents, all parents, who love their children, for all parents who strive to help their children navigate life's highway. I intended it to help smooth out the bumps for them. Is that not what we are all after?

I grew up in an almost perfect world, shielded from sadness and harm by two wonderful parents who loved and adored me. We probably were considered upper middle class. I thought that we were rich, at least, relatively rich. Maybe we were. There is no way that I could have ever been prepared for what awaited me. My world was probably like every other middle class girl in the South, who graduated from high school, attended college, found a husband, and settled down to raise children. I am sure that all of you are familiar with the 'Cinderella Complex', as it is called. I saw life through rose-colored glasses and it was beautiful. I have always been an optimist by nature and that has stood me in good stead wherever I go. The only problem with all of this was that I went to work. If I had just worn my little apron, kept to my recipes, changed those diapers, 'tended my oven' as Sarah Vaughn sang, and worked for the PTA, what a life I would have missed!

I have tried to tell you in this book about the various states and realities of the world of my mind. I describe my awareness of these and how I roamed in and out of these realities. I have tried to convey to you the sadness, the sweetness, and the horror that filled many of the youths that I encountered. My cup overflows with these youths I was trying to help. I hope to enrich your life with my experiences.

Now where did I put that pencil? I need to write these things down right now as I think of them because once they fly through my head, that part of the reel may not rewind again!

To start this off with a copied poem seems a little strange, I know, but this poem came across my desk recently and perhaps it was what started me reliving the past years. A student in a high school in Arizona wrote it. I wanted to share it with you.

Now I sit me down in school
Where praying is against the rule
For this great nation under God
Finds mention of Him very odd.
If scripture now the class recites.
It violates the Bill of Rights.
And anytime my head I bow
Becomes a federal matter now.
Our hair can be purple, \orange or green,
That's no offense; it's a freedom scene.
The law is specific, the law is precise.
Prayers spoken aloud are a serious vice.
For praying in a public hall
Might offend someone with no faith at all.
In silence alone we must meditate,
God's name is prohibited by the state.

All are allowed to cuss and dress like freaks,
And pierce our noses, tongues and cheeks,
They've outlawed guns, but first the Bible.
To quote the Good Book makes me liable.
We can elect a pregnant Senior Queen,
And the 'unwed daddy' our Senior King.
It's 'inappropriate' to teach right from wrong,
We're taught such 'judgments' don't belong.
We can give out condoms and birth controls,
Study witchcraft, vampires and totem poles.
But the Ten Commandments are not allowed,
No word of God must reach this crowd.
It's scary here I must confess,
When chaos reigns the school's a mess.
So, Lord, this silent plea I make:
Should I be shot; my soul please take!
Amen

The shootings at Columbine High School in Colorado made me revisit my life and made me feel that I had something to say that most people who had children would like to hear … maybe not, but I am going to say it anyway. The events that led up to the shooting of the young people and the horror of the shooting itself filled my mind with memories of a lot of the young people that I came in contact with through those thirty years.

For over thirty years, I have had the privilege to be with young people in a counseling situation in a couple of high schools in Eastern North Carolina. I was a Biochemist first and a Counselor second. I returned to graduate school at the tender age of forty and received my masters in guidance and counseling. My mentor in my first job was Raz; an ex-marine turned principal who thought that I had the common sense that was so often missing in counselors. I entered the counseling field with a B. S. degree in Biochemistry and 13 years of work in basic research in the Medical School at Duke University. I did not have one counseling course in any classroom anywhere.

Before I start this book, I need to talk to you about all of the students at my two schools. The majority of them were bright, with good families. The book would seem to imply that all of the students were poor, parents were nonexistent and all of them were eaten up with problems. I have presented the students that I have because of their uniqueness and the need for people to understand them. These kinds of students usually find their way to a counselor so my experience is generally with them. Although I have talked to perhaps thousands of students, these are not expected to represent the general population of students at the schools. This book represents my experiences and my world. Care should be taken in extrapolating them further. I will discuss this further in the last chapter.

CHAPTER 2

Getting Started

The educational system calls what I did 'lateral entry' and anyone can do it as long as they are attending school somewhere to become certified in the area that they are going to work in. Stupid me!!!!!! I started working on my counseling degree the same year that I became senior counselor in a high school that integrated for the first time with a student body of 25% American Indian, 40% Black, and 35% White. Now let me tell you; a white woman with a middle-class background has not the vaguest idea of the ethnic backgrounds of two of these races. To someone who was born in the South in the early 30s, a black person was a maid who lived in your house, cleaned, cooked and took care of you. Someone you loved, but someone that you knew nothing about. You knew nothing about their feelings or desires, hopes or loves. An Indian! Well that was someone who wore a headdress, carried a hatchet, and was killed by the soldiers in blue coats along with the buffalo.

It was only later that I did a little research on the Lumbee Indians who filled that school and found out that they were thought to be the remnants of a tribe that lived on Hatteras Island, North Carolina, in the 1500s. It was thought they were the tribe who took in the Lost Colonists when their food and supplies ran out. That tribe was then called the Croatan. Today the descendants are known as the Lumbee tribe. The name was changed to Lumbee in 1952. They were named after the Lumbar River that flows through Robeson County. The name Lumbar sounded very hard to the Indians and they always called the river the Lumbee, hence their name. When they were first discovered, they were living in houses similar to European-style homes. The houses had doors and roofs. They were farming in the European manner and they told about white ancestors. They had English-sounding surnames and some of the people had green eyes and light brown hair. There are now over 44,000 members of the tribe and 90% of them live in Robeson County. North Carolina. They are the largest Indian tribe east of the Mississippi River and the ninth largest tribe in the United States. Enough of that!

School opened on a hot, sultry day in late August before the time of air conditioners. We did have electric lights but little else. My office had a glass window in the front and was about 10 by 10 feet. I guessed that the glass window was so that you could see out into the main office and waiting room. My fellow-counselors consisted of one large, large Indian and one small black lady. Both of these counselors had been transferred from the segregated schools where they had been a counselor in the previous year. I know that you are not going to believe this, but we counselors had not met until the day school opened. I had a large bookcase in my office but I did not have any books. I could have brought all of my science books but I did not think that they would have come in handy for this particular line of work.

On that first day, I had on my prettiest cotton dress and high heel shoes. I was blond, blue-eyed and very fair. I was thirty-three years old and I thought that I had the world by the tail.

The first order of the day was homeroom and there was a homeroom next door to my office. We heard all of this screaming and screaming and it sounded like they were coming through the walls. My only thought was to help somehow stop the fight that was obviously out of control. I ran with the Indian counselor into the room. Two boys were on the floor going at it. He pulled the top boy up and I remember stamping my foot and screaming at the boy on the floor to get up. I think the idea of this stupid white lady wading into that scene and stamping her foot at them did more to calm their tempers than anything else that happened. They stopped fighting and I knew instinctively that this fight was because they were afraid of each other and did not know what to expect that hot day in August. One of the boys was black and one was an Indian. Blood was streaming down their faces and both boys had razor blades taped between two fingers, two razor blades to a hand. This made the blades out of view unless the students opened up their hands. As I looked around the room, I knew that most of the other boys in that room on that day also had razor blades.

I said very loudly and in as stern a voice as I could muster, "Anyone else found with these razor blades will be suspended for the rest of the year". I did not know whether this was true or not, but I felt in my heart that it must be. Fear was what started the fight. I could see it in their eyes. Fear of each other, fear of the unknown!

Their clothes were ripped; both boys were crying and I was horrified. By this time, the room was full of teachers and the teachers marched them off to the principal's office, blood flowing

The principal! Oh yes, the principal! What a man! He was crew cut, hard nose, ramrod back, and the personification of the stereotype of the marine that he was before retiring.

The second thing that was on the agenda for that hot August morning was a general assembly. The principal wanted to tell the students what he expected of them. It was held also to let them know how tough he was and that he meant business. All 1600 students filed in, found seats, and the magnitude of all of those students in one small area just left me speechless. The Principal stood up and said, "You may NOT wear heavy chains. I see them everywhere. A boy may NOT wear his hair longer than one inch from his scalp. If I see anyone with hair longer than that, I will personally take them to my office and shave his head! A girl may NOT wear her dress shorter than one inch above the knee. If I see a skirt shorter than that, I will personally take her home and tell her parents that she had broken the school rules. Anyone caught fighting will be suspended for the rest of the year. Anyone who brings a weapon to school will be put in jail and tried on a weapons charge and be suspended for the rest of the school year. They will not be allowed to enroll in any school in the state of North Carolina for the rest of the school year and will carry a criminal record with them for the rest of their lives. The rest of the rules, I will make up as we go along and if you don't like them, too bad."

"*Damn,"* I thought. "*How can he possibly enforce those rules?*

The students were all from rural or small towns and I was still in shock over everything.

The teachers had met thc day before and had planned a skit so that the students could get to know them and everyone wanted it to take some of the edge off the situation. The teachers had all practiced it the day before.

It was time for our skit and my part was to do the '*funky chicken*' out to the middle of the gym by myself, although I had not practiced it. Each teacher was to do a different dance and we changed dress for the part. I bet you do not know what the funky chicken is. Well, it's a dance that resembles a chicken flapping its wings. You move your elbows up and down in a flapping motion. And your feet? Well God knows what your feet do. Whatever it was, mine did not behave that day and right before I got to the middle of the gym, I fell flat of my face. I went spread eagle on the floor. That completed my first day of counseling.

Every day, for the next two years was just as eventful. Remember I told you earlier that I found out why I was hired. Well, it turned out that my job was to go before the principal with the student and act as a buffer and enabler. I was to beg for a lighter sentence for the student or try to talk the principal into letting the student off since it was his first offense or whatever defense the situation provided. The principal put on his tough man act, used his loudest voice, and I was to help him save face. He would scream at me just as loud as he screamed at the student. He and I should have been on the stage since it was such a beautiful act. The funny thing was that he and I never discussed this staging but I knew that he knew that I knew and he knew that I knew.

A lot of times there were teachers in his office who had brought the student in for this or that and his voice would come over the loud speaker in the guidance office, "Mrs. Jones report to my office (you know that Jones is fictional). One of your precious babies is in trouble again." It didn't really matter whether or not I knew the student. I would always pretend that I did and it always ended up with the student in my office and a wonderful counseling situation would ensue. As a counselor, what more could you ask for? It was building a wonderful reputation for the guidance department and the students thought that I walked on water. This is not to say that he always made it easier for them, but it did make it easier than they thought it would be after he got through screaming at them. It got to the place that he didn't even have to call me, the student would ask for me.

I remember reading, somewhere during this time, a report put out by the *Public School Forum of North Carolina*. They had conducted a study that was begun with an analysis by the Meyers-Briggs personality assessment of some 600 principals who had attended the "North Carolina Institute of Government's Principals' Executive Program" in its first eight years. More than 70% of the principals had profiles that indicated they tend to be more comfortable with the status quo and less than open to change. Surprisingly, perhaps, there were few differences among the principals when the data were analyzed by age, sex, years of experience, or race. Only 28% had profiles that indicated they were visionaries or catalysts for change. There was at that time mounting evidence that transformational leadership - leadership for change - was key to the success of school reform. I think that this is still true today. Thank goodness that Raz was there. If there was anything that we needed to meet the challenges of that school, it was change.

He probably shaved the heads of 10% of the boys in the school that first month but they finally caught on and they all had the cleanest haircuts you have ever seen. Some threatened to sue, students' rights and all of that stuff. Yes, we had some parents who came up and wanted to mouth off at him. He would scare them so badly when they came that we never saw them again. I know that you are saying that we never had just the right one or they would have burned the school. I think you are wrong. I think that deep down they knew what he was trying to do. They knew that he wanted a safe place for their children to go and the kids knew it. Most of them did not want their parents to interfere. Don't forget that we were unsophisticated in the ways of the world. For a lot of those students, that hot meal at the school was the only food that they had during a day. It was the only warm place for them in the winter and the only roof over their head when it rained.

No student wore a heavy chain around their neck, no girl wore a short dress to school, and no lawyer with fancy ways tried to sue him. We still had fights, he still suspended students for the rest of the year but they were that 1 percent. The rest of the students were perfect. The different colors didn't eat lunch together or like each other but they existed in the same confines with each other and the situation didn't boil over. It was explosive but somehow he held it together. Alternatively, perhaps that is a "we".

Now I told you about our trips to Raz's office, well, let me go into that in a little more detail. Raz had this old swivel wooden chair, you know the kind that you can turn around and around, and it goes up and down. It also had a hinge on it that would let you lean way back, I mean way back. Seeing him in this chair was my first encounter with 'non-verbal communication' and what a lesson it was. I had only been working about a week when I had my first encounter with him in his office like this.

He would sit in that chair and prop his feet on his desk, he was about 6'2" and weighed about 190 pounds and when he got all stretched out with his arms behind his head and almost horizontal, he was a very imposing figure. Every time that I saw him that way, I was sure that his chair was going to tip over backwards but it never did. Now can you imagine how a little student felt looking at that imposing figure? I was always surprised that they didn't wet their pants and I am sure that some of them did. I just didn't see it.

This was back in the days when jocks chewed tobacco, and just for effect, he had a tin can sitting by his desk that he would spit tobacco juice in every now and then. He would just sit like this for the longest kind of time, just spitting, and sitting and everybody in the room was afraid to say anything. Most kids would begin to sweat and in his booming voice

Raz would say, "Is this kid one of yours?" without even looking at me. Sometimes my voice would even squeak when I answered. I don't care how many times I visited his office; this sight always scared me.

No, Raz and I did not have a sexual relationship, as I am sure that you are thinking right now but we probably could have at a different time in our lives.

Did you know that educators did things like this? Did you know that they tried to make the transition from authority in the home to that at school as firm as possible. They try all of the tricks in the trade. I once knew a teacher who told me that every year he placed a trash can on the floor next to his desk so that he would pass it as he walked to the chalkboard. Right at the first of school, he would kick the trashcan on purpose, and knock it over, spilling all of its contents everywhere.

He would scream out in the loudest possible voice, "God Dammit!" Who put that trashcan there? You had better tell me right now. His goose is out of here." He kept fussing, fuming and threatening everyone in the room for the rest of the period. He never had a discipline problem the rest of the year ... tricks of the trade they call it.

I guess this is as good a place as any to tell you about the BIG Indian counselor. He has a prominent place in many of the other stories that I want to tell you. He stood about six feet four and God knows how much he weighed. His belly preceded him about eight inches when he walked. It was not a jelly belly; it looked very firm, just big. He drank a lot of beer but not in school. He told me he did anyway. He was about the slowest man I ever met. Nothing rattled him. He always went slow and easy and he thought slow too. Not dumb slow, just slow. He had these jet black eyes that had no light in them. You know the kind, they look into your soul and you can't see yourself. Sometimes I would get lost in there and couldn't seem to find my way back. I have never been hypnotized, but I am sure it is the same kind of thing. Sometimes when I looked, I forgot what I was going to say and it would take me awhile to get my thoughts together. I could just imagine how a student felt when they looked in there.

He would swagger out of his office real slow like, with that belly preceding him, and everybody would stop what they were doing and look up. You couldn't help it. He just commanded attention without even realizing it. He was like the educated blacks in those days, in that he had no patience with Indians who didn't try and he constantly berated them. He wouldn't give them the time of day. Most of them started coming to me because they knew I was a soft touch and would mother them to death.

He would laugh at me and say, "White girl, you got a lot to learn". I thought he did too but I didn't say so. We made a good team when it came to dealing with young people though and we knew it.

One of the best descriptions that I could give you of him was the day that the water pipe broke in the guidance office. The water was gushing out and filled the office in no time. My Indian Councilor, Gerald — Oh, I forgot to tell you, his name was Gerald Maynor — came walking out of his office real slow-like with the water almost up to his ankles. His pants were dragging along and he had his hands in his pockets. I was running around like a chicken hopping about and almost in a frenzy.

He said, "Now girl, you ain't paying for this water, what are you so excited for. We ain't going to float away". He picked me up, sat me on top of the desk, and said, "I know what it is. You don't want to get those pretty little shoes wet. Now calm down and let's see what we need to do."

Raz, Gerald, and I made a formidable trio. When anything big was happening, Raz would come and get Gerald and me and off we would go to meet whatever it was head on. Like the day they had the first football practice! The Black coach was worried to death about mixing up all those colors and he knew he would not be able to field a team because they wouldn't play together. After Raz got through working on them verbally, you know togetherness and all that stuff, and I got through mothering them, sweetheart this and that, and Gerald cussing them out; well that year they won the state championship. Maybe it was because they were so mad at each other. Who knows, but they never fought each other and they learned a lot of respect for each other too. Children are so resilient. If only adults were!

Now Gerald was a different kind of fellow. He talked so low that even I needed a hearing aid. I sometimes thought that he did it so that the students would have to sit real still to hear him. He would look down at you from that huge body and it seemed that his gaze would go right through you. Boys didn't back-talk him or muck with him. They knew that he meant business and he only said things once.

I saw him with a student one time that had tried to give him a little sass. He grabbed the boy's lips in his thumb and forefinger and pinched down on them as hard as he could. As he was holding them, he looked down into the boy's eyes and said. "Do it hurt? If I ever hear you say anything like that again, I will pinch your lips off." Strange punishment wasn't it? But, he was from a different world.

I think that this might be the perfect place to inform the reader that no school system can operate without the people who teach in it being what the system calls team players. Everything that someone does depends on somebody else there helping to make it work. If you are testing, you've got to have someone to help you give it. If you've got a discipline problem, you gotta' have someone referee for you. If you want to talk to a parent, you had better have someone with you. If you want to do some classroom guidance, that teacher better like you or you are out of luck. If counselors think that they can walk into a school and be an island unto themselves, they have another thought coming. Because, believe me, you need that teacher more than she needs you until you establish yourself as a helper. You had better do everything that you can to make them feel good about themselves if you plan to have a good guidance program.

CHAPTER 3

The Children

Now back to my students. One of my worst memories involved a wonderful, beautiful, Indian girl. She came to me in my office with the glass window and told me all about herself. She told me how she was in love and how she would kill herself before anyone would make her stop seeing her boyfriend. I immediately thought he must be either black or white and she was crossing the boundary lines. During this time in my life, I had not learned to ask the right questions. That came many years and many students later. Anyway, after talking to me for about an hour, she blurted out that she was pregnant and that her father would kill her if he found out. Remember, at this time, I was counseling out of my back pocket so it seemed very logical to me to give her all of her options, abortion being one of them. We talked on for another thirty minutes and she said that she would be back tomorrow. I encouraged her to tell her parents and pointed out that they would soon know anyway. She was about three months pregnant at this time.

The next morning I was filling out some never-ending paper work when I heard a commotion in the outer guidance office. I looked up to see a middleaged Indian man putting his fist through the glass window in my office and pushing through my door. He had the biggest knife in his hand that I had ever seen and he was coming straight at me! Remember, I told you about that BIG Indian counselor that worked with me, he saved my life that day and I ended up with only a minor cut on my arm.

When we finally got the man calmed down after he had been de-knifed, it turned out that he was mad at me because his daughter had told him that I said she should have an abortion. Now you know and I know that I never said that but the student thought that it was in her best interest if she told her father that and he came after me. I learned another valuable lesson that day too. When you are a listener, and in the helping profession, being quiet to some people means consent. Don't ever forget that. Learn how to use it early and learn the right 'uh huh's' to say when and where. Learn the right head shaking too. It's very important. I am not sure that we ever convinced him that I had not said it but he had vented his anger and after he finished crying over the virtues of his daughter, the three of us had a good counseling session and I learned, probably for the first time in my life, how red men and fathers feel about daughters. Underneath, we are not all that different. It's a shame that some people never have the opportunity to find this out. What a privileged life I have led!

We were having some group counseling sessions at the beginning of the school year to try to help the students adjust to each other. I had a really good group, with all colors present and I was following some printouts that were developed by some university somewhere. One of the questions was, 'If a black, a white, and an Indian were drowning and you were on the shore and could only save one person, which one would you save'? Pretty heavy question, isn't it? I can promise you that I was totally unprepared for the answers that I received from that group. The question was given to them one day and they were to think about it that night and read the answer that they had written the next day in class.

My education continued when the next morning the question was revisited and one of the Indian boys said without hesitation, "The white person of course". I found out much later that counselors are trained to register no surprise at anything a student tells you. If you show surprise on your face they know immediately that you disapprove or that what they have said is so out of the ordinary that you can't believe it. Strange, isn't it? Your body language is very important because students read that at once, all of them, but I digress. The Indian boy said, "You don't believe me, do you?"

When he said this, there were five students in the group, every student who was not white immediately said, "He's right, that's what we put down too." I figured that all of them would have put down the one of their own race. It turned out that they did not think they were worth saving when you compared them to a white person. Does this blow your mind? We walk around thinking that everyone thinks like us, but believe me very few people do. How do you think your life would be if you felt you were inferior to half the people that you came in contact with? Belligerent, angry, incensed, I can think of a whole string of adjectives, all of them bad, that would fill my mind.

What did the two white people say in the group? "The white person, of course."

My newfound 'old' friend from today wants to argue about this. He says that it can't be true and I am making it up. I told him just like I told you earlier, that's the way it happened. I am trying to keep this honest and I have to say just what happened. I don't care what people say or how much they believe it, but that's the way it was then. Perhaps it would be different today and everybody feels that they are equal to everybody else but I doubt it.

We spent two weeks, an hour a day, talking about that one question. There was no way that I could erase the inbred feeling the students had, but perhaps I helped to raise their self-worth a little. This attitude came up all the time during my counseling career.

Black students who had the opportunity to attend things out of the rural or small town school setting like Governor's School in the summer or Leadership Camps or campus trips to Universities would come back saying, we were so surprised to find out that what we thought and had to say was important to someone else. They learned that their ideas were worthwhile. Does that have something so say about what white teachers were teaching black kids in those days? Perhaps even today in some classrooms? Alternatively, is it learned in the home and can't be erased;

only hidden at times. Do they lapse back into it at the least provocation? I can't answer that question for sure. I only know that I have never seen it completely disappear.

I was blessed with the gene to catch on pretty quick to what was going on around me. Some people would call it intuition but I knew when a fight was going to erupt even before the students did and believe me they knew everything. Their grapevine was something else. I think people don't ask them things because they don't really want to know. If they trust you, they will tell you everything. I don't mean trust you not to tell, I mean trust you to do right by them. This is a mistake that many counselors make; sometimes they want you to tell. You just have to know the difference.

Raz's voice came over the intercom in the guidance office. "To my office, both of you!" We knew who he meant.

"We got weapons on campus according to one of the bus drivers," he said as soon as we walked in. Those words were enough to chill anybody's blood who works in the public school system. I had felt for a couple of days that something was going down but I was not sure what. By lunch, we knew that it was coming out of the black community. Something or other from the weekend carried over to school. By two o'clock, a black girl had been knifed in a classroom, dead at the scene. Another black girl on the run. You have heard of the Hatfields and the McCoys. Well, we knew that everybody who ever knew or was related to either girl would have to get in on the act. Raz went on the intercom and told them to be sure that they killed each other off the school ground. He would not tolerate fights in school and he would suspend anyone forever who started one. He said he did not care who killed whom off the school ground. Looking back, I am not sure what it was that kept the lid on, but keep it on he did. That night, houses were burned, people killed, but not in school. It was almost as if it was hallowed ground. Perhaps somewhere underneath, they all knew that education was their only hope. Perhaps not!

The Indian boy who walked into my office looked disheveled and hollow-eyed and had given the secretary a hard time when she asked him what he wanted to see me about. Her smart-assed remark made him even more hostile. "You'll never get a note from me to get back in class unless you follow the rules," she spat at him.

Every public school student and everybody who has ever been a public school student knows about that coveted note that excuses you from the wrath of the teacher. It behooves every counselor who ever works in the public school system to know the difference in a student who is just trying to get out of class and one who really needs to talk to you. You may think that you walk on water and the whole world of students is waiting to see just you, but it probably is that you are a soft touch and they know that they can con you. It was years after I retired from counseling that I was told by one of my students that the only reason that he came down so much was to look at my legs. Furthermore, his class was boring.

I have a very distinctive handwriting, left handed and all that, and in thirty years of counseling I never found but one student who could copy it. All of the teachers could spot a forgery right away and many a student went to after-school suspension for attempting to fool the teacher with a copy.

Anyway, I had told that secretary a dozen times that we were in the business of helping students, not hassling them. It was to no avail, and there she went again. I knew that I was going to have to talk with the other counselors about her before it was all over. No guidance department needs anyone in it playing the smart-ass!

The boy sat down across from me at my table. I never sat at a desk during the whole thirty years that I worked with young people. There is something about a desk that reminds students of authority and they are less inclined to talk to you, and you sure can't help them unless they tell you what is wrong.

"I can't sleep anymore. I haven't slept since the Fed people moved us into our new house", he blurted out. "That air conditioning, heat, and those hard floors. It's not like our old hut with dirt floors and no heat. I have always slept on the floor and these floors are just too hard. I just can't get used to it. What am I going to do? I want to go home. I keep a cold and my eyes run water all the time. We are all unhappy. They bulldozed our old house down. Momma told me to come and talk with you. Maybe that white lady could do something", he said.

How selfish we are to think that we can impose our middle class values on others with no care for how they feel. Whoever could imagine that someone would not want a free new house! After many meetings and much conferring with the Feds, we finally resolved part of the problem. The Feds were talked into buying beds, mattress and chairs with some of their blood money for all of the Indians that they had moved. They also agreed to set up classes for the women to teach them how to use their new appliances, how to raise their windows, and all about modern living. It turned out that they did not even know how to turn their lights on.

Well it wasn't long before the electric bill came due and when they couldn't pay it, the electricity was turned off and they were right back where they started as far as lights and somewhere to cook was concerned. I revisited that area some years later and I was not sure that they had ever adjusted to their new life. Some of them had shoveled dirt on the floors to make them feel more at home. They were still cooking outside over an open fire and using the woods as a bathroom. I know that it is not like that now but it was then.

As I told you before the Indian's tribe name was Lumbee and they are a very different lot. They are very set in their ways and none of them like change. Most of the Lumbee Indians have very green eyes and the theory is that they are direct descendents of the Lost Colony on Croatan Island, North Carolina. I don't know about where those green eyes came from but they are so green that you are startled when you first see them. They were very addictive people. Alcohol, cigarettes, and over-eating were rampant among them. I want to say that they were lazy but they really were not. It was only that they moved slow and thought slow. They liked to say that they were communing with nature and sometimes they were. They were not much into school work. They had a whole lot rather fish and it was hard to tell when they were smart. Teachers had a hard time with this and when they got to fussing at one for not doing his homework, the student couldn't understand why the teacher was so upset. Who cared; they didn't have any electricity anyway so once darkness fell they couldn't do their work and I am sure that there was not a teacher in that high school who had ever visited an Indian in their home.

You know, there was a very good series of books out then to help you run a group session on how to study. 'Every student should have good study habits if they are to do good in school,' the series stated. One of the sentences in the book said, and I am paraphrasing, 'First find a quite room away from the family, preferably with a desk. Be sure that the light falls over your left shoulder on the book or paper that you are working on.' It never said that it should fall over the right shoulder if you are left landed but I guess that is a true statement. I, myself, am lost in a right handed world. One day, lefties are going to take over. Now how relevant is that study habit to a student who lives in a one-room shack with no furniture and no electricity and has six or seven brothers and sisters? It only makes them acutely aware of what they don't have.

I never came up with any answers for the Indians' problems but I understood them. I guess they had been subjugated for so long that they just gave up. They retreated into a land of mysticism and dreams of what might have been. There were a lot of stories floating around that told of all the land that the Lumbees once owned. Then, as land grew scarce, they were falsely charged with theft and made to pay fines that they could not pay. Then, the land went to pay the fines. When the land was gone, they were made to work off the fines by being 'bound out'. They were auctioned off on the courthouse steps in Lumberton, a town in Roberson County, to the highest bidder. Their children were taken from their homes and bound out to work in the white man's homes. All of this for the good of the children according to the court system. The children were just free labor.

As late as 1958, the Ku Klux Klan invaded the town of Maxton in Roberson County to terrorize the Indians and run them out of the territory. However, the Indians banded together and forced the Klan out. Later in this book, we will cross paths with the Klan again but that is another story. Indians have always had trouble in that county. I know that you remember in the 1980's several Indians were killed by sheriff deputies and the Indians retaliated by taking over the Newspaper and holding hostages. I was not there then but some of my friends told me about it

To my amazement, they practiced all kinds of voodoo with dolls, wooden sticks and incantations. It was nothing to see one come into the guidance office with a doll with pins in it. It was a replica of someone they had fallen out with and they were casting a spell over them. Usually it was a teacher. This was very serious business to them and not something that you joke about. I remember that it was during this time that the first American landed on the moon. There was no question in their minds about that. The pictures were staged by the American Government to make the public think someone had landed on the moon. It was not real. They always hated anything about the Government. There was nothing that we could do to make them believe that a space ship had actually taken someone to the moon. I guess that they still don't believe it. Superstition is a powerful thing and it prevents education from taking place.

CHAPTER 4

The Problems are Serious

I encountered my first case of incest at that school. This was back in the days when you didn't have to tell Social Services anything unless you wanted to or felt that they could help. Regardless of what anybody tells you, when kids get high school age, Social Services is a joke. They will probably put me in jail for that remark but it's true. The girl was thin beyond belief. She had long stringy hair and what my Daddy used to call that hangdog look. She walked stooped over and never looked anyone in the eye. When she told me how her daddy climbed into bed with her at night, ran his hands all over her and raped her repeatedly, I could not help but cry for her. Anal and oral sex were his favorites. I had never even heard of anal sex at my tender age. She said that she bled all of the time. She was only sixteen.

There have been so many times in my career that smoke would get in my eyes, or so I would say, and when smoking would no longer be an excuse, my allergies would act up. I have never been allergic to anything in my life but it was a good excuse to use a Kleenex. She described how it made her feel; how her Mother knew but would not do anything about it and preferred to pretend she was lying. She said that she cried all of the time but she had nowhere to go. She was the oldest of four girls, and oh yes, she was white.

You know what I am going to tell you, don't you? You know that I talked her into letting me talk with her father. Somewhere in my warped mind, I thought that he might stop if he knew that I knew. I could think of no other way to help her and my heart ached. Back in those days, listening was not enough for me. I was too young and too hot headed.

When he came to my office that day, our conversation went something like this:

"I know what you are doing with your daughter."

"Oh, it's none of your business. I own her. I feed her. She sleeps in my house at night. I buy her clothes and pay her bills. I will do whatever I want to with her. If she talks with you again about it, I'll kill her."

"You do know that incest is a crime and you could go to prison for sleeping with her."

"Is it?" I really didn't know whether it was or not. I knew it was something that you just didn't do but past that I was ignorant. He said, "This conversation is over!" He got up and left. I guess that I was lucky that he didn't blow my head off.

Next, I called the mother in. I just couldn't let well enough alone. Do you know what she said? "Sure, I have known it all along but I don't have anywhere to go either. So what's so wrong with it? He puts a roof over our heads. I don't have to work and he is good to me. It also keeps him from worrying the hell out of me, so I just ignore it."

So much for my first incest-counseling job! I did call Social Services but nothing ever came of it. The girl was sixteen. The magic number!

But I digress. Let us talk about Velma. She was white, seventeen, short, and pretty. I had never seen her around school much. She was not involved in anything that I knew of. I had heard some of the boys snickering about her. Some said that she was an easy 'lay'. Some said that she didn't have the sense that a billy goat was born with. I was never sure how anyone knew how smart a billy goat was, but they must have thought it was pretty stupid.

"Ms. Jones", she said. "I need someone to talk with. Nobody at home ever listens to me. I think that I am in love and I am not sure what love is. I know how busy you are and this will only take a minute."

I look at all of the paper work stacked up on my desk and hate the people who forced me to have it there. The reports, the transfers, the tests, the proof of being accountable, everything that administrators require to make their job look important. I sometimes thought that if we could do away with the county office and all that they represented, how wonderful the school could be.

Velma and her problem was crisis counseling. It's not how a counselor should spend their time but somehow, during my career, I found it absolutely necessary. You just have to make time for it. You had better make time for it. To hell with all of it, I thought, and I pushed it aside to make room for Velma's elbows.

"I have been dating this boy," and she called his name. It was a boy that I knew. He came from the best side of the tracks, as some people call it. Others call it rich. "He says that he loves me and he wants me to have group sex with some of his friends on the football team after the game on Saturday. He says that if I don't do it, he will know that I don't love him and he will stop dating me." Remember, you can never look surprised at anything that you are told if you are good at what you do and I was trying so hard to be good and to keep from going out and killing that boy. "He and I have been having sex for about six months now. I have never met any of his friends but I feel that they are important to him." I felt that this conversation was straight out of some movie that I had seen. The one where the boy ends up killing the girl because she got pregnant and he had another girl on the hook. I forgot the name of it.

"Do you want to do this?" I asked.

"Well there isn't anybody at home who listens to me, or pays attention to me, or cares whether I live or die. They fuss all of the time and there's so many of us living in that trailer that I hate to even go home. He's the only thing that I have. He's the only one that cares about me."

Now where do you go from here? What can you do to make this precious child feel loved, wanted and special? Nothing! Nothing that I hadn't already done. I listened, I empathized. I cared. We talked, and talked. We even started a group session with some girls that she felt had the same sort of problem. She did not go that Friday after the game, I know, but whether she could stand the pressure that he put on her later, I don't know. Later I would see this group of girls eating lunch together and talking and I knew that I had done something good. They had each other to lean on. Before, they had no one.

As my mind travels back to each one of these incidents, they are as vivid in my mind as if it were yesterday. The faces of the people, the words they said, even the inflections in their voices come quickly to words on this page and I wonder what makes it that way. Was it the time in my life, or was it the fact that the experiences were so new and phenomenal to my closed mind? Perhaps it was my awakening to the world around me. In those years, most of the women that I knew had the Cinderella Complex as it was later described. You know, go to college to find a man, marry right out of college and have children, never work, never explore, and never think. If you graduated from college and didn't marry that summer, you were considered a failure because women didn't work. You had to go home and live with your parents. Heaven forbid.

Right before school was out, a black man and his son came into my office. I recognized the boy. He was the one in the fight at the beginning of the year with the razor blades taped between his fingers. The boy had been out of school all year and the father pleaded for me to go and talk to Raz with them. What they did not know was that he could not have been kept out of school the following year even if we had not wanted him to come back but sometimes what you don't know won't hurt you. It was important that he felt we were making concessions for him if we were to keep him in line. I never will forget how humble the father was and how convinced he was that he wanted his son to graduate from high school, but not with a GED. He had only finished the sixth grade and his son was the first one in his family that had come this far. The boy was contrite also and spent a great deal of time telling me how sorry he was for all that had happened. He was a good boy but as I told you earlier, he was scared.

We do strange things when we are afraid. He had the feeling that he was marked forever, and he was, but not for the reasons that he thought. I cried, one of the million times that I cried, over things not being fair, over life's injustices, over people who can't help themselves, just over life as it was presented to me every day for the next thirty years.

People in that town were afraid. Afraid to attend ball games, afraid to come to school programs, afraid to go out at night. They were even afraid to come to PTA. It was the beginning of a new school attitude that still exists in some areas today, almost thirty years later. Everyone said that parents did not come to school because young people did not want them there. Students had reached the age that they didn't want their parents involved. That was not true. The white parents were afraid, the Black and Indian parents did not feel comfortable there and I can't say that I blamed them for that. Therefore, we just rocked along with only teachers and students at all school functions.

White people have always been afraid of black people. They have never taken the time to get to know them. To some whites, blacks all look alike. It might surprise the whites that the black people feel the same way about them. We smell too and it's not a good smell to the blacks. We have always associated black with fear: the black list, the black night, the black witch. It goes on and on. The word black is ugly and fearful.

I will tell you right here that I think that it is very difficult for a white teacher to teach a black student. The reverse is also true. It is very difficult for a black teacher to teach a white student. As for the Indian, he's lost from the very beginning. There is nobody to teach him. I am sure that the educational system would rise up in arms over this statement but I believe it with all my heart and all my soul. I am talking about teaching so that the student rises to their fullest potential. What the blacks should have marched for is equal funding rather than integration. They removed themselves from their neighborhood and their teachers. They were put with teachers who did not love them and did not know how to get their attention. How can you teach someone when you cannot get their attention? The blacks began to feel that it was not 'cool' to study and make good grades and any black who did was cut off from their race, ostracized by the group. They had nowhere to go. Those days were bad indeed for the intelligent black. I think that it still is.

I don't think that things have changed too much today. Racism and prejudice are still ugly realities in all sectors of American life, including education. Racism may be less overt than in the past, but its effects can still greatly harm minority students. I even wonder if subtle, insidious forms of racism could be more harmful to young people than the more blatant forms. Prejudice against the poor is another force that works against the academic achievement of disadvantaged students.

It's not only teachers who need to examine their expectations for students; administrators must also be held accountable. Counselors need to consider whether they are steering students into undemanding courses because they are poor, minority, or female. The expectations that all students can achieve at high levels, under the right circumstances, should be the guiding principle of every school. Sometimes I felt we should have mapped out a four-year plan for them from eighth grade on and not even let them have a say-so in what they took. Do you think that it might have helped? I know that we would have had a lot more failures. Should we have just let them fail and repeat. It always amazed me that we just kept doing the same old thing even though it didn't work. We keep repeating the same experiment over and over while hoping for a different result.

I am trying to keep this book as intellectually honest and as close to the truth as I can possibly remember. All of the incidences that I talk about actually happened. These students are real. Some of the things that I talk about, you will not believe. On the other hand, you will feel that I made up some of the people. I did not, and I can only hope that the people that I discuss will not see themselves in a light that I did not intend. They are all striving every day to do the very best that they can. Some are misguided, some have no background on which to lean to make decisions, and some have no role models. None of them are bad or mean or amoral. The schools do have that kind of student but they are not the kind that I had the privilege of talking with.

I have a problem with who my customers are for this book. Is it counselors in training, teachers, administrators, parents? Even students crossed my mind. I really don't know. I do know that young people touch all of our lives in every way imaginable and all of us deal with them at every level of our lives. We deal with them as parents, grandparents, teachers, peers, administrators, businessmen, associates, and even jailers. The more that we know about them, the better we are able to help them or guide them along some sort of path, over what my mother called '*Learner's Hill*. That is a hill that everyone must learn to navigate. If we make bad decisions, we fall back. However, with good decisions, we climb higher. Being a teenager means climbing, climbing, until one can reach the top and go over it. Perhaps I will call this the information book into teenage problems. I don't know the answers, but I do know the problems.

Young people get to the top of Learner's Hill but it is on fragile wings. These wings may not be strong enough for them to reach the top. Learning is what being a teenager is all about. They are all facing challenges and travails from which they must learn to make good decisions. We all breathe a sigh of relief when we feel that they have reached the top and have achieved a meaningful adulthood.

I keep thinking about how to tell you what counselors are supposed to be doing for young people in a few words that you would understand. Now, I am talking about high school counselors only. What they do or should do is not the purpose of this book and I am sure that you will hear me say this on every page. I can probably best describe the essence of their work by saying the following: some students make inappropriate decisions based on a variety of reasons. The counselor tries to help them see that inappropriate decisions lead to behavior and emotional problems. They want to help students develop alternatives, along with responsibility for their actions. They use a variety of methods to accomplish this. Now I can go on and on about all the strategies, plans of action, and talk your ears off about this. However, I will only touch on some of these as I am telling you about my students and telling you about my students is what I want to do.

I will go out on a limb here and say that I personally feel that over half of the teenage problems that I encountered occurred from severe depression in young people. I feel that teenage depression is a very real crisis in many families. Problems of truancy, trouble at school, drug and alcohol abuse, sexual acting-out, pregnancy, running away from home, and even suicide all seem to be related to depression in young people. Most people who deal with young people expect them to act like adults when they are depressed, sad, lethargic and tired. A depressed teenager, on the other hand, may seem to be extremely angry and rebellious. Hyperactivity is also a reaction against depression. It is almost as if their emotions are discharged through their actions.

The real problem is that the destructive potential of serious teenage depression has long-lasting after-effects. There are numerous things that prevent a young adult from having a full, healthy, productive life. These include dropping out of high school, having and keeping a baby, getting into trouble with the law, sustaining a serious injury as the result of risk-taking behavior. Then there are the physical problems that drugs or alcohol cause, car-related problems and many, many more that I won't name here.

For example, when a high school girl who gets pregnant decides to keep and raise the baby herself, about 90% of her life is already written for her. Freedom is reduced just when it should be increasing. Dreams go unrealized, often forever. She usually spends a lifetime under-educated, unskilled and living in poverty. Most black students will not even consider abortion and my feeling is that a lot of them set out to get pregnant. They see parenthood as a way to recapture the joy of their childhood that they have lost. Some of them have expressed it by saying that they will then have someone to love them. They will feel wanted and accepted.

Let me tell you about one of my students that I will call Darla. If this dialogue sounds unrealistic to you, it is as near the actual conversations that she and I had as I can make it.

Darla was black and on the low side of the intelligence scale, real low, and had been raised by an unmarried mother on welfare. She had three or four siblings, all I think, from different fathers. She came into my office one day and said that she had been considering having a baby. She had a pencil and paper in her hand and she said, "Ms. Jones, please help me out. I am trying to figure out how much it will cost me to have a baby and I have come up with the following things. A big bag of pampers will cost about $xxxxx and I will breast-feed the baby so I will not need to buy baby food or formula. The school will send out a homebound teacher so I will not fall behind in my schoolwork and I could be back in school in about three weeks. The check from Social Services will be about $xxxxx a month and all of the medical bills will be paid for by Social Services. I will have someone to love me and make me feel that I am great and I will have money left over to spend on me, something that I have never had."

Now I ask you, what do you think that my chances were of convincing her that things were not like they seemed and that they did not add up to one neat little package like she thought they did. Her chances were slim to none. I said all of the right things to this wonderful girl who had nothing, but to no avail. We talked, talked, and talked some more. I even ended up reading some facts to her. She could not read very well. In the end, I thought that I had made a little headway. The only headway that I made was to act as a sounding board for her to bounce her ideas off. I saw her about four months later and she was pregnant with twins! I thought about her calculations and her lack of money for the second pack of pampers. I thought about the hopelessness of her life, her role models, and the fact that she would have someone to love and to love her; and I cried again.

One morning when I arrived at school, I found two girl students and a teacher sitting on the guidance sofa. Both students were disheveled and dirty. One was a freshman and the other was a junior. The teacher pleaded with me to talk with them before school because neither one of them needed to be in class. I knew of the family and I knew that the father was a driver for an eighteen-wheeler. The story that unfolded was one out of a fiction novel. It would have made a wonderful movie.

The father had returned home from a long haul drunk as he could be, probably hyped up on some kind of drugs too so that he could stay awake. He was screaming and running about the house and hitting at the children. He found his shotgun and told them that he was going to kill all of them. They all took off to the woods and as it turned out, they spent the night there because they were too afraid to go home. He was actually shooting into the woods where they were. When morning came, they just went to the bus stop and came to school on the bus.

There were four children; the other two were in elementary school. The name of the oldest one was Judy. She was seventeen. As she told me about her night from start to finish, my mind raced ahead of her story to try to find an answer. There was none, I knew it. I knew it as well as I knew that I was sitting on that chair in front of that precious child listening to a story that tugged at my heartstrings.

I am sure that I have told you this before somewhere in all of these pages but you cannot get Social Services to interfere when a child is sixteen or over, which almost all of the high school students were. I asked the oldest girl to call her mother and have her come up to the school to talk with us. The mother was at work and she couldn't come but the father answered the phone. What a cussing he laid on me! He was trying to get some sleep and I had awakened him. Well, needless to say, by the time that he got to my office he was the kindest, sweetest man that I had ever seen. He loved the children, told them how sorry he was that he had frightened them and that it would never happen again. Drinking had made him crazy, he said. He wanted them to come home with him so they could get some rest. He said that they didn't need to be in school after being up all night.

Oh, what misgivings I had when that man walked out of school with those two children, but my hands were tied. What could I do? I knew in my heart that this episode would not be the last. The next time that he took off on a long haul, the same thing would happen when he returned. How long could the children put up with that kind of behavior. Would he actually kill them one day? After lunch, I received a call from the counselor at the elementary school where the younger two children attended. She told me that the younger children had told her the story and she had reported it to Social Services. I knew the scenario well. Social Services would visit the house and then tell the parents there had been a report of child abuse. The parents would deny it. There would be no proof. The father would be screaming mad at the children for telling someone about it and threaten to kill them if they ever did it again. It would be the last time that we would hear anything from the children and they would live in that mess until they could escape and get on their own. What madness!

The other side of the coin was just as bad. Social service would remove them and put them in foster care and they would stay there no longer than two weeks. They would then be crying to go back home because they missed their parents so much. A fact of life is that children adjust to their situation and love their parents regardless of what they do to them. Crazy isn't it? The thing that really makes you cringe is all of those trucks on the highway with you, driving eighty or more miles an hour and the drivers drunk or high on something. Every time that I see a truck, I think about those children.

I never saw those children again. None of them ever graduated from high school and I never heard anything else about them. It was as though they disappeared into the woodwork. Vanished!

Graduation time came at the end of that first year, and as I watched those young people walk across the stage that night, I was so sad. They were going out into the world with such great expectations and a great many of them did not have a Chinaman's chance in hell of ever having a job with any better pay than working in a fast food place. The middle class whites got so bent out of their frame at the whooping and hollering by the audience when certain names were called during that solemn occasion. I must say that it made me happy because I knew what some of them had been through to get a family member to that place in their life. It made me want to holler too. The white people had never understood the 'free spirit' of the blacks anyway.

The fact that we had even gotten to that place ourselves that first year was still an amazement to me.

I now had four graduate courses in guidance and counseling under my belt and that summer I took two more. I learned that we had a developmental guidance program in our high school. Let's go over that 'what a guidance counselor does' again, in the very briefest of words. I will give you the definition that I learned. Developmental guidance attempts to meet the needs of all students, addressing the typical concerns, questions, and choices facing young people. They learn about interpersonal skills and relationships. They learn how to take an active part in school, to set goals, to develop study skills, to make responsible decisions, and to solve problems. Don't we all wish that we had learned to do that somewhere along the way. This book is not about learning to be a counselor; it's not about all that I learned in graduate school; it's not about all of the styles of counseling and how you learn which is right for you. It's about young people and how they cope with what they have. It's about telling you about them. We must go on.

CHAPTER 5

The Second Year

The beginning of the second year was much easier, maybe because we knew what to expect, maybe because the students were not as afraid. My BIG Indian, Gerald, did not want to be senior counselor because he did not want to deal with all the white parents. Most of the students who went on to further education were white. Does that surprise you? Therefore, I took the job again. In all honesty, I wanted it. I liked students that age, I liked to address the kind of problems they had and I enjoyed helping them decide where and what they were going to do in the next phase of their life. I didn't have a problem with the white parents. They thought that I walked on water anyway. It was all of that certainty that flowed out of my mouth. I was not lacking in self-esteem. As I told you before, I thought I knew it all. Looking back on all of it, I realize how stupid I was.

As senior counselor, another big part of my job was college placement and career counseling. Now that was easy. All you had to do to be an expert in that field was to be able to read and I did my homework. This was the area where you could make the parents love you without doing much. I knew all of the admissions people in every college on the eastern seaboard before the year was out and was on first name basis with them. I could tell you what every college offered and which one had the best program. I could sit and talk with a student for 30 minutes, look over his record and tell you exactly where he should go to school. I could tell you where he would succeed and where he would flunk out without some help. This is not saying that I always told the parents that. You know how some are, they want you to get the student in where they want them to go. Take the SAT twenty five times, redo the class rank, anything to get them in that prestigious school. Find someone to give them an individual intelligence test, move heaven and earth but get them there. I could do that too before it was all over.

I learned all about financial aid, how to get money for a student, where to go for scholarships, and I can truthfully say that all that a student had to have was the will. I was responsible for the way. It became a 'thing' with me to know about every scholarship there ever was and how to get it. I could fill out financial aid papers blindfolded, but the students were my love. You have to set priorities but I was never good at that.

I inherited the gene for letting the words flow from my mouth with feeling.

Sometimes, even when I did not know what I was talking about, the people listening were convinced that I did know. I think that somewhere along the way it was called 'letting your personality show when you are talking.' Some people even go so far as to call it charisma. All of the Civic Clubs, the PTSAs, the garden clubs, the churches, everywhere that more than five people met wanted me to talk to their club. Talk I did, every chance that I got. To hear me you would have thought that we had the best school in the world, everything was rosy, everyone loved each other, and it was all a breeze. We had the best principal in the country, the best guidance department, and the best teachers. You have to have the parents on your side. You learn early that perception is the thing. If your senses tell you that something is good, it isn't long before you begin to believe it.

You are saying to yourself now that I have not mentioned the black guidance counselor. I didn't forget her. But, I didn't like her. That wasn't because she was black. I just didn't get along with her. Perhaps the thing was that I didn't respect her. She had this thing on her shoulder that she was just screaming for someone to knock off. She had been queen bee in her black school and now we had integrated and this bitch of a white woman who didn't know anything had taken her place. I don't blame her; I would not have liked me either. Understanding where she was coming from did not make me like her any better. I know that 'where she was coming from' expression is trite but I use it often to indicate background, culture, rich or poor, and other formative or causative circumstance. We were always at cross- purposes. She contended that I did not understand the blacks or the Indians and I was trying to play God. As I saw it, she didn't understand anybody and that was the truth. If the real truth were known, nobody liked her. She was the bitch, but in the end, I turned out to be one too. I told Raz that I would not work with her anymore and at the end of that first year, Raz fired her, on my recommendation, and we got another one just as bad. I have heard that most people go into counseling because of some trauma in their own lives that they cannot resolve and I must say that a lot of the counselors that I have known fulfill this prophecy.

There was a teacher in that school that loved to back students into a corner. She was a home economics teacher and back in those days, both boys and girls took home economics. Isn't that wonderful! Have you ever noticed that most home economics teachers are straight-laced, humorless and never smile? I have known a lot of them in thirty years and they all follow the straight and narrow. Everything is black or white to them. I guess it is all those recipes they have to follow so closely.

My office was about two doors down from her classroom and sometimes when I was in the hall, I could hear her raving and ranting at the students. I would thank my lucky stars that I did not have to sit in her classroom. Every day she banished some student somewhere, to the office, to detention, to after-school study hall, to the guidance office anywhere to get them out of her class. Of course, it got to the place that they would act up just to get out of her class.

One day she went too far and the student came back at her full force. They got into a fistfight in the classroom and all of the students went crazy, screaming and carrying on. Gerald and I broke it up and drug the student down to guidance. We both knew that he was a goner but I guess that we were hoping she would not swear out a warrant on him. You know, assault and battery. We sat and listened to all the things that she had done to him, how she had belittled him in front of the class. How she had called him stupid, lazy and ignorant. How she had called his parents 'trailer trash', that's when he came at her.

We walked with him to the office so that Raz could expel him. We said some asinine platitudes like, "You are going to have to shoulder the responsibility of your actions. It's your right to defend your honor, but you must suffer the consequences." Now isn't that a lot of help to a kid who is getting shipped out, perhaps put in jail. Especially when we thought that it should have been the teacher to get shipped.

I was so mad after the shipping and calling his parents. You know where I went, straight to the teacher's room. School was out by then and I felt like fighting her myself. There was nothing that indicated that she felt any of it was her fault. I begged her to sleep on it before she did anything that would harm him for the rest of his life. As you know, anger makes you do strange things, and I thought perhaps that if she waited until tomorrow, she might feel differently about the punishment. She didn't and there went another student down the drain, one with no hope for tomorrow.

I guess that I need to say here that because the culture of most minority students is different, they are often misunderstood, ignored, or discounted. The minority students are likely to experience cultural discontinuity in schools. They get out of 'sync' as Jacqueline Irvine stated in a book that she wrote in 1990 called *Black Students and School Failure*. Teachers must understand the backgrounds of the students that they are teaching to avoid this culture clash. I could not agree with her more. It is demanded that most minority students leave their culture at the classroom door and behave like the white students. If they don't, the teacher and the student clash and confront each other, both consciously and unconsciously. How in the world can a student learn in a situation like that?

Do I sound liberal to you? I looked up the word liberal in the dictionary and the definition was: "as an adjective 1. generous, 2. ample, 3. abundant, 4. not literal or strict, 5. tolerant or broad-minded, 6. favoring reform or progress - as a noun, one who favors reform or progress." I am a liberal. I say it with conviction. I scream it to the heavens. I want to reform teachers into believing that students are human beings. I want young people to have a second chance. I want adults to listen to them and believe that they are worth teaching to be responsible members of society. I want everybody to realize that young people have to climb that 'Learner's Hill' and it takes some longer to get to the top when they have no one to show them how. This is not a political conviction and has nothing to do with politics.

This book is not about meeting the needs of students from diverse cultural, ethnic, linguistic, or socio-economic backgrounds. I could talk about that forever. Reams of books have been written about that. Everybody has a theory. Having watched the educational system meet this problem over the past thirty years, I am as sure as everybody else who has a theory that my theory is the right one and I will state it here and never again in this book. Remember that it is only what I believe.

Principals have consistently placed their worst teachers with the low achieving students. These are the students who do not seem to care or do not seem to have the ability to do the work and consequently cause discipline problems in the class. This sets up the student and the teacher for failure from the very beginning. This happens from the first grade on through 12 years of schooling. Teachers fight for the top groups. Parents refuse to accept bad teachers for their students whom they consider bright. They hound the principal, hound the teacher; they move heaven and earth to provide the right atmosphere for their children. They take their student to private consultants who give their children tests to make them eligible for top groups. These are the parents who are educated, affluent, and involved. What does the parent do who either works two jobs for their children to go to school, has no car, or doesn't care about education in the first place? You know, they accept that bad teacher; they don't know the difference anyway, and some don't care. These parents don't feel comfortable when they come to school. They feel like everyone is looking down their nose at them and they are easily brushed aside.

These students do not know how to teach themselves. They do not know self-discipline and have not been taught how to learn, how to think and solve problems. I guess, if you want to put all of this into fancy words, you would say, 'effective teaching traditionally provided to the most privileged students must also be provided to students who have, until now, been academically marginal'.

I guess that this is a good a place as any to talk about '*grouping*'. Now those of you who are not in the educational network may have a problem defining this word. Let me define it for you. It is a dirty word and depending on what year we are talking about, it either means putting all like children into the same classroom or on the other hand, it could mean messing them all up by a secret formula, or it could mean random assignment. How's that! Well, I have lived through all three types and I am still unsure of the best way. At the present time, we are dead set on catching up the lower-performing students by giving them extra classroom instruction (together) and material they can handle. On the other side of the fence, we are dead set that our best and brightest will not be held back by having low achieving students in their classroom.

The achievement gap is major. In 2000, the U. S. Department of Education reported that by grade four, African-American, Latino, and poor students of all races were already about two years behind other students. By grade 8, these same students were about three years behind other students. Does it surprise you, knowing this, that 90% of Whites and 94% of Asians complete high school while only 81% of African-Americans and 63% of Latinos, in the same age group earn a high school or GED diploma? Furthermore, one-in-50 Latin and one-in-100 African-Americans 17 years old can read and gain information from specialized texts such as the science section in the newspaper compared to 12-in-12 Whites.

I have already told you what I think the biggest reason for this is. We moved them out of their home culture, out of their neighborhood. There is a disconnection between their home and school and they are no longer in a familiar environment. We are trying to make them reject their cultural identity. Most of them do not care whether they achieve academically or not. Back to the '*grouping*'.

When I started off in education, the best and the brightest were separated in the classroom and we now have come full circle and are back to that. It did not work thirty years ago so what makes everyone think that it will work today? I am at a loss for words.

I am a scientist by nature and education. I am a big believer in genes, and heredity and I know that there are some things that you cannot change. I also know in my heart that environment must play a part somewhere. I once read a wonderful book called *Nature or Nurture.* I forgot the author's name, but it made a lasting impression on me in that it presented both sides of the coin so effectively and the research to go along with it. It forced me to include more of the environmental possibility in my thinking.

One day Raz showed up in my office door and told me to get my coat we were going visiting. He yelled for Gerald and the three of us took off to one of the senior's houses. The student had not been in school for about a week and the family did not have a telephone. Now I have never been one to visit the homes of my students. First off, you never know what you are going to meet there and most of the students don't want you to go. They want to keep home and school separate, somewhat like church and state, you know. I thought that maybe they didn't want me to see where they lived and I knew that they didn't want me to meet their parents. Anyway, we go streaming out to this kid's house to find out what is wrong with him. The fact that he did not have a telephone told us a lot.

He lived way out in the county, near the river, out in the woods. We noticed that there was an outhouse and that the house was about to fall down, in fact one section of it had fallen down. We got out of the car and we must have been a sight to the man who came out of the house with a shotgun. The big Indian, the big white man with the crew cut, and the little white girl all dressed up in her high heels! My mother always told me to dress my very best every day because you never knew whom you were going to meet and I always did. That was right up there with always wearing clean underwear because you never knew when you were going to be in a wreck and have to go to the hospital.

The man told us to get off his land but Raz walked right up to him talking all the way with the gun pointed right at him and he told the man we had come to find out about Raymon. Raz took the gun away from him and pushed him back in the house. Raymon was lying on an old cot in the one-room house with a dirty blanket over him. Raz asked the man if he had seen a doctor. "Don't believe in any old doctor", the man said. "We use witch doctors up here." I felt the boy's head and he was burning up with fever. He was barely conscious. Gerald leaned over, scooped the boy up in his arms and carried him to the car.

He died that day, about an hour after we got him to the hospital. It was pneumonia. What a waste! A week earlier, he could have been cured. He could have '*walked the walk and talked the talk*' and probably lived a productive life. Who knows? He might even have been president someday. What a sad day. If only we had gotten involved three or four days earlier we might have saved him. I never forgot him. When you get in these big schools like we have today, sometimes you get lost in the shuffle and fall through the cracks like Raymon did. Every school needs a system in place to keep track of things like that.

I remember a movie that they showed us many years ago at a teachers meeting. I think that it was called *An Angel In The Snow,* or something like that. It was about a young boy who rode a school bus and it was snowing one day when he got off. He fell in the snow with his arms outstretched and no one knew who he was. Not a soul on the bus knew his name, not even the bus driver. It was so sad and all of us cried and cried. Everybody who works with children should be made to see that movie. Just like every teacher should be made to see the '*The Breakfast Club*'. Now there's a movie for you! It's all about school detention on Saturday morning and what really happened to all the students who had to go.

I use to wander how Raz would have fared today in our school systems, with lawyers on every corner just licking their chops for a lawsuit. It has always seemed strange to me that all of the laws are made to protect about 1% of the student body when the other 99% have to sit around and be inconvenienced because of them. What happened to the majority rule? Why do special interest groups get all of the attention?

Why does the majority sit back and let themselves get walked all over? It's a puzzlement to me.

I have had a lot of dealings with handicapped groups through the years and I have always been an advocate for the students who needed special attention. I would always move heaven and earth to see that they received the attention that they needed. I could tell you tales that would curl your hair about some of them. Their parents are always angry. They generally vent this anger on the teachers who teach these students. What they are really angry about is the fact that their child is different and they want to know 'Why Me'? There is no way that a teacher can give individual attention to a handicapped student in a classroom. The benefit comes from the child being with other students, being accepted with their handicap and being a part of something.

Parents want the teacher to give them all this extra stuff in the classroom at the expense of all of the other students. They want individual instruction and demand it amid threats of reporting the teacher to the State Handicapped Whatever. It can't be done. I don't care what anybody says, it can't be done. Teachers can smile and say, I will, but they can't. There have been millions of books written about teaching children with learning disabilities in the elementary schools but few have addressed a high school situation where you have 40 students in one room and a student with severe disabilities like muscular dystrophy, cerebral palsy, or autism. These include spina bifida, or epilepsy, or paralysis in the arms and legs, or congenital malformations. That teacher has to answer to end-of-course testing and students must know their course work or she will lose her job. Where would your responsibilities lie in that situation?

It's very simple to the teacher. 'If we make all of these accommodations for struggling students, won't it hurt them when they get into the 'real world'? Isn't there a time when they should learn basic skills without the aid of technology or extra help? Where will they find adult environments in which such deference is paid to their special needs?' I really feel that teachers need only be concerned that these students leave school feeling confident that they can learn and that they are worthwhile members of learning communities. When they feel that way, they are much more likely to make their way successfully in the 'real world'. Acceptance is the key. A teacher's job is to accept that student with all of their disabilities into that classroom and into their hearts.

I don't think that the average parent realizes how many of these students are in our schools. Neither do I think that the average school realizes how many parents would be willing to volunteer days to help the school with those students. Most principals are afraid to call in parents to high schools. It's almost like they don't want the parent to know what is going on in their school, what the teachers are teaching. This valuable resource has been untapped in my opinion for the past 30 years. Perhaps it lacks an organizer. There I go again, getting off the subject, forgetting my objective and lecturing. In this day and age, lecturing is for the birds.

There was not a white boy on the football field or a white boy on the basketball court those first two years. When my wonderful family would go to games, there were no white people on the bleachers except the few whites who attended school there. My beautiful white daughters would sit with all of their friends of various colors, who were also beautiful, and my husband would fume. He could not accept any of it and I knew in my heart that we would have to leave. I also knew that it would come soon. I was not prepared for how soon.

Everyone in that small town felt that Raz had done such a good job in the high school that he should be the county superintendent. I knew that he would never placate all of those people. I did not feel that he could survive in that environment. He was not the type to compromise, to go to the meeting table, to attend luncheons, to talk at clubs, to work on budgets, and to keep everyone happy. He gave orders. Everyone was supposed to salute and keep in line. I talked to him about this but he felt that he could do more good for the students from that vantage point than anywhere else. It was announced about three months before the end of that second year that he would be moving up to the county office and a new principal would be named for the high school. I always wondered if there had been a lot of complaints made by the parents about his high-handed tactics and they were removing him from a really hot situation. I was not 'in on the know' at that level but the thought did cross my mind.

My husband found a job at the end of April in our hometown, the town in which we grew up. He went to work there by the middle of May and we stayed until school was out. Then, away we went to another life. I often wondered how it would have been if we had stayed there. However, you cannot dwell on what would have happened; you have to move forward and meet that new day. I kept in touch with Raz and Gerald through the years. Life was good to my big Indian, Gerald. He became Dean of Students at The University of North Carolina at Pembroke. This school was established in 1887 for Indian children to receive an education. They did not have a school to attend until that time. Today that small Indian school has received full status as a university and has been incorporated into the North Carolina Greater University System. I know that Gerald made a good Dean of Students. Through the years I had a great many students attend that university and I would always send them to Gerald.

Raz did not make a good superintendent. He succeeded in making everyone in the county angry with him and was isolated for a great many years. I was invited to attend his retirement party about ten years after I left but something prevented me from going. I would have loved to have seen him and talked over old times when we were both young. I had not heard from him in over 20 years but writing the early part of this book made me think that I need to go back there and see him. I only briefly saw him when we both received similar awards decades later and I did not even recognize him

CHAPTER 6

The New School

The rest of my years were spent in a high school located in the town that I grew up in, married in, and raised my children in. I sat in the church every Sunday that I, my father, and both of my children had been baptized in. Both of my girls and I had been married there in the same dress. Half of my friends that I spent my time with had graduated from high school with me. To say that I knew everyone in town was an understatement. I knew most of their parents too.

The high school routinely graduated around 350 students and generally had an enrollment of about 1500. There were only grades 10 through 12 when it first opened. To give you some idea of the times, we did not have a copy machine, so when students applied to college I would have to type a new transcript each time they applied to a different college. About 45% applied to college. We did have part time guidance help. The lady who did it was probably seventy years old. There were three counselors, one assistant principal and one principal. The school had integrated the year before and half of the student body had boycotted graduation because they felt they had been persecuted. Maybe they had.

As soon as I found out that we were leaving, I called the principal of the new school and told him that we were moving to his town and I would like to have a job in his guidance department. I told him to call Raz, gave him the number, and told him that I would bring my resume and documents when I came to meet with him. As you already know, I was green and I didn't know that you were supposed to go through the county office and they sent everything to the principal in the county who needed a counselor. I just knew that I wanted to work in that school and it seemed to me that the principal who ran the school was the best place to start. Raz must have convinced him that I walked on water, because the next day I had a call to come up and interview.

I put on my best summer dress, my high heel shoes, the same ones that got the water treatment, and I am convinced to this day that if I had been ugly, I would have never worked at that school. That's why I like men so well. They appreciate good-looking women and respond appropriately. Deliver me from a woman boss! I have had one and it is not a picnic. I was destined to spend the next twenty-eight years in that wonderful school with its wonderful children, wonderful parents, and its wonderful teachers.

When I look back on it, I think that I made a difference and that is a feeling worth savoring. He did not need a counselor, he did not have a slot for one, the state had given him a slot for another assistant principal, and he hired me in the place of that assistant principal. For those of you who do not know, hiring administrative people is all about slots. You get so many slots in the administrative end for each student and back in those days principals did not like guidance counselors. Most principals were ex football coaches and when the era of the big consolidated school came in, most of them were lost. They were not accountants, not business oriented; they did not know anything about curriculum, about organization, about testing and testing was just rearing its ugly head. However, I am getting ahead of myself.

I must set the stage for you. The guidance department consisted of one white lady who was probably sixty. She was senior counselor and her name was Elma. She had come from a very small school when the schools integrated the year before. They had moved four schools together from the northern part of the county and some of the students, who were bussed in, spent about an hour and a half on the bus coming and an hour and a half going. All of this was done in the name of integration and racial balancing. What a shame for everybody concerned. I think that the law says now that you cannot keep a student on a bus longer than an hour. Can you imagine how it was for a parent whose child wanted to participate in after-school activities, like football, to get that kid home after practice?

This lady was a witch, complete with broomstick. She had these deep black eyes that looked right through you. They were set deep in her head too and seemed to come at you from a tunnel. Her hair was mostly white, wiry, and stuck out in all directions. She was big and made a big impression towering over you. She had been senior counselor and you can imagine how she felt when the principal walked in and told her that I was taking over that job. She was to counsel tenth graders. Boom! Just like that, she was demoted and replaced with this whippersnapper that did not even have her Masters Degree in the subject. She was still going to school and she was young. Elma was straight off the farm and walked with both feet flapping out. Her clothes looked like they had been her mother's and there were times that I know that she wore the same dress for three days. Either that or she bought three of the same dress each time she went shopping. The story was that she and her husband had the first dollar that they ever made and owned oodles of acres of land.

Now you know that the seventy-year-old part-time secretary was her buddy and sided with her. Between the two of them, they tried to make my life a living hell but it didn't work. They gave me the silent treatment. I didn't care. I didn't want to talk with them anyway. They tried to alienate the students, but the students would rather come to me. I was somebody different and they didn't like the witch anyway. They started a gossip campaign among the teachers. The teachers, thank God, did not believe them. It went on and on until they finally gave up. It took too much effort and they were old. I would be old one day too and I knew it even then. What am I talking about? I am old now!

The other counselor was named Edna. She was typical of the blacks in those days. Often seen but never heard. She was somewhere between forty and sixty. I don't think that I ever knew her age. In the twenty-eight years that I worked with her, I never saw her without a wig. I really liked her but what she did in her office all of the time was a mystery to me. She ate in there and spent all day in there, never with many students. Back in those days, the blacks wanted the whites to tell them 'what was what' because they thought we knew everything. They also knew that we had more influence in the whole system than the blacks did. There were more of us too. The school had around ninety faculty members and of that number, no more than nine were black. How did they get away with that? I have no idea. I was told that, when they integrated, the principals were responsible for keeping the teachers that they wanted and the county office was responsible for moving the rest around as best they could. Thirty-five percent of the students in the school were black. No Indians anywhere to be seen. The Mexicans came later, much later. Most of the black teachers that were kept were Cracker Jack teachers and I liked all of them.

I must introduce you to the principal also. He was an ex-football coach who had made a name for himself coaching. He was tough but at the same time, very sensitive to what people said about him. He could blow up in a minute but calm down just as quick. He was nice looking, with black hair and very sensitive hands. He was about 5'10", slim and I will say around 45. I was never very good at guessing people's age. He would tell off someone in an instant and once wronged, he held a grudge forever. He expected everyone to work nine hours a day because he did. His family came second to his job and if the truth were known, I am not sure that he liked any of them. His wife's mother lived with them and I sometimes got the feeling that he did not want to go home. It took many years for him to realize that he could not run that school without me; and, the relationship to begin with was nowhere near the one that I had with Raz. There were many times that I wished that I was back with Raz and I missed the security that I had with my mentor.

I had attended summer school both sessions the summer before I started working there and I had only two more courses and my dissertation to finish up that degree. I think that I knew what I was doing as much as anybody did in the field and a lot more than most.

I started out wooing the teachers because I instinctively knew that I would not be able to do much without them on my side. As I have told you before, no guidance department is any better than the support that it gets from its teachers. With them on your side, you can move mountains. I did things like having little coffees for them early in the morning, once a week. We would talk about the problems they were having the week before and about the students who were acting up. I kept these meetings small so that they would feel comfortable talking about the students. I rotated them through the whole faculty. I tried to give them pointers on what they might try with those students and I would always follow up. Following up with them individually was the key. They had never before had anyone do that. I would give tests in the classroom for them and would do group guidance when they had somewhere to go. I know what you are going to say, but I don't care. I was not setting myself up to do things that I would not be able to keep up. I considered these things in my job description. See, I had learned a lot that summer. I even knew that I had a job description and could pretty well outline it for you. I never went off campus for lunch; I never left work early; and I was always there early. I knew I had to give them the impression that I worked as hard and as long as they did. I worked harder in most cases. Elma and Edna left when the bell rang and that is the kind of thing that they were used to.

When they had to meet with a parent, I always met with them and acted as a mediator for them, a buffer so to speak and they loved it. It got to the place that I was counseling them as much as the students. I went over all of their test scores with them and explained what they meant and what they needed to work on. I acted as a buffer between them and the principal, sometimes to my own disadvantage. He took it out on me many times when I was taking up for them. The one thing that I never did, and if anyone reading this is going into counseling, don't ever forget, I never sat for a class when the teacher needed to be out. Once you do that, they will always call you and there are a great many teachers who will abuse you. I was always busy with my stuff when they asked me. You can get by not doing that if you do other things for them.

I courted the vocational department. They always hated counselors and felt that the counselor gave them all those bad students that they had to teach when nothing else was left to put them in. Some of that was true. I helped them do registers when they didn't know how. Most of them in those days were what we call lateral entry. They worked in an area outside of the school and the school system could hire them to teach young people hands-on work in their field. Take a mechanic for instance. He probably had worked as a mechanic for some automobile company right out of high school for a couple of years, and was hired to teach students how to work on cars. These kinds of people knew their stuff but knew nothing about students or how to teach out of a book. They were the lowest ones on the totem pole in the school hierarchy. Nobody gave them any respect.

Speaking of registrars, that was a book that homeroom teachers had to keep to let the office know who was absent, who dropped out, who enrolled and when. It had to be kept very accurately and everything had a number. Each page looked like a calendar with little boxes that you marked. Everything had to tally up, number of students present and number of students absent had to match total enrollment less dropouts on any given day. Oh well, it was complicated if you had never done it before. Once you got the hang of it, things had a way of falling into place.

Perhaps we need to talk a little bit here about '"my" South, my area that I was born and raised in and what I had walked into during this second part of my counseling career. To know the child, you must know where he or she came from and the family that raised them; you are then almost home free.

It's hard to explain about the South because it's really the mystic South, the allegorical South. It's a region of the mind. What do I mean by that? Stereotypes or preconceptions that we have of the South really refer to "pictures in our minds" rather than reality. Think about it a minute. When someone says the South, do you see a moonlight and magnolia world with everyone sitting on the porch drinking a mint julep or sweet tea? Of course, you do, and you see *darkies* in the field singing and belles wooed by slender gallants. The movies, the books written, and the plays all have helped perpetuate this idea. Even the Southerners themselves believe it. The myth itself authenticates customs, rites, institutions, beliefs, and is frequently directly responsible for creating them.

We all recognize the Allegorical South where literature defines reality. So many misconceptions and literary devices have been used that we accept almost anything as the reflected reality. I call this the Allegory of the South. Plato's Republic introduced the Allegory of the Cave where chained prisoners only saw shadowgram reflections of life and thought that portrayed reality. These anomalous observations distorted true reality. The Allegory of the South presents shadowgrams that simplify the world by casting false images. Such literary giants as William Faulkner, Margeret Mitchell in *Gone with the Wind*, Tennesee Williams, Eugene O'neal and others generate the Allegory reaching for reality. I think I can also see *Uncle Tom's Cabin* down there, and there's Mark Twain's *Tom Sawyer* and old Huck Finn rafting down the Mississippi. Even the movies give us *Tobacco Road* and *Deliverance*. The allegory reaches a point that anything said about the South is believable. Moreover, it is believed.

Admittedly, some of it is true.

Part of the South's unique appeal lies in the love and commitment that Southerners have to family and kin. When you picture a southern family, you think of them sitting on a front porch at twilight, swapping stories. Maybe they are eating fried chicken for Sunday dinner around the kitchen table. There are long visits from maiden aunts and distant cousins, black maids waiting on the family and sometimes becoming in effect family members. They are attending church and Sunday school every Sunday and attending prayer meeting on Wednesday night. Don't forget the family rituals such as births, weddings and funerals; each is an occasion for homecomings and celebrations of kin. These myths about the power of the family group in the South rest largely on the experiences of white residents in small towns. In truth, that was what my area was.

Southerners love to fight! This fact is born out time and time again by my students. They love resolving interpersonal disputes with violence. Whether truth or myth, Southerners seem to have monopolized military enlistment. They provide disproportionate support for our wars. This occurred in both World Wars, Korea, Vietnam, Iraq and all American military endeavors. Why someone even wrote a book and said that the reason that Sherman burned the South was to teach the women of the South the horrors of war and to keep the women of the South from sending all of their children to war because they were over-aggressive and they thought that it was their patriotic duty. I said myth or truth; "my" Southerners think that it is truth.

Search your mind for just a minute and tell the truth. When you think of the South, do you view it as a land populated by stock characters? Do you see rambunctious Good Old Boys, demagogic politicians, corrupt sheriffs, country and western good old girls, cheerleaders, football All-Americans with two first names, bible-thumping preachers haunted by God, sugary Miss America candidates, and toothless, grizzled "poor white trash?" Perhaps you do not see this in your mind's eye, but the South does; they see themselves that way. I remember reading somewhere, a long time ago, and I can't give the author credit because I cannot remember who it was, "that the stereotyped South is a country on the mental map of the national imagination, its citizenry a distillation of both fact and fiction." I love that and I have always remembered it. My school was in an area where all of those characters existed. I saw them every day. They walked in and out of my office and in and out of my life.

My small community of 10,000 people, and that's an exaggeration, is so conservative that they squeak when they walk. When you travel outside the city limits on any one of five different roads leading out of town, you are struck by one glaring fact. If you started counting houses versus trailers, even today, trailers will probably outnumber houses. You are also struck by the fact that the land is so sparsely inhabited. Great vast areas of woods stretch for miles with nothing on them but trees and underbrush. Why, you ask? There is nothing to do anywhere around but farm. That's the next thing that glares back at you. Tobacco barns once stood proudly on the land, but no more. Barns in every state of disrepair blight the landscape. Some are half fallen with vines growing in and out and roofs missing. Some are flat, with the roofs sticking up. Some have sides missing. In fact, if the truth were known, you would probably have to travel thirty miles or more to even see a barn that was still in use. The individual farmers, who once made a decent living selling tobacco in one of the eight warehouses in town, do not exist anymore. Twenty years ago they were all sharecroppers, or tenant farmers. They rented the land for crops from landowners or tended the land for landowners, always growing cotton in my youth but the big crop was tobacco. Then they starved to death.

Not literally, but after the government extorted billions from the tobacco companies and put them under attack, the farmers had to find something else to do. They left farming in droves. Fortunately for some, industry had begun to trickle down to "my" South .They abandoned their barns and embraced industry. This meant a better way of life for some and some continued to do small farming on the side, so to speak.

They did not abandon their old customs and ways. The country store and their church are still the site of most of their social gatherings. The church was not for the sermons on the subject of eternal damnation, but more as social centers and communication sites for community news. The glue that held it all together was the schools. Schools prepared the young ones for maturity and the world. It taught them about decision-making and the Y's in the road that must be faced. It prepared them for jobs, for further education and for lives. Schools and the church were the social glue.

Integration took their community school away from them and they have been mad ever since. They were mad even to the point of ceasing to be involved in school functions. Even in the face of the migration to industrial jobs in industry, there are a lot of customs and human interest areas that will never be replaced. These include a love of sports, a taste for regional foods and cooking, a streak of religious fundamentalism and the love of a good folksy story. Have I painted a picture that you can understand? I hope that this will help you see where my students are coming from and why they act as they do.

CHAPTER 7

Homeroom and the Klan

The reason that I became so professional at counseling then was that I got a homeroom. This was a designation of a number of students over which I had responsibility. We met each morning and prepared for the day like the other homerooms. Counselors do not scream! It was the only way that I could get what I wanted for those special students who needed every subject that they were taking to graduate. It was the only motivational tool that we could find that would make them work and to tell you the truth, it was the only way that we could keep up with them. This homeroom was able to go with the other senior homerooms and do everything that they did even though they needed seven subjects to graduate. The other seniors only needed from one to six depending on the number of courses that they had passed. These students were unmotivated, always in trouble, tired most of the time, and had failed at least three courses a year since enrolling in the ninth grade. Most of their parents were on welfare and they all got free lunches. Ninety percent of them were black. There were so many of us that we had to meet in the auditorium. Usually, I had around 46 students, give or take a few who dropped out along the way. It consisted mostly of males and the black girls that were in it were usually pregnant with the second baby.

They were the roughest, toughest bunch of young people that I had ever seen but I was never afraid of them. They treated me like a queen and they knew that I was doing something for them. They were also very protective of me, as I was of them. 'Don't muck with her students', was the word on the street. I would go into the auditorium at 7:30 every morning in the dark; I never could get it through the thick head of the janitor that we met in there for homeroom. I would feel around behind the curtains for the lights and by the time that I got them on half the class was there.

It was during that first year that I was on the way to the auditorium and two of my students were walking in front of me, a boy, a girl and me. You know how things happen so fast that your mind does not catch up with what you see. Well, it was like that. In my mind, I thought that the girl had just run her hand down the back of the boy but in fact, she had laid his back open with a razor blade. It was not until the blood started running down his back that my mind caught up with my eyes. By this time in my life, I was pretty calm about most of the stuff that happened. I could do what I had to do initially, and fall apart about an hour later. This was definitely an improvement. I steered the boy back to the office and called an ambulance. The girl took off running. There were no EMS's or 911's around then to help you out of tough spots. We only had the police, the fire trucks, and the ambulance. I had learned something a long time ago. The blacks only cut up their friends or somebody they know. I knew the girl who did it and now I had to get to her to have her turn herself in before I had to tell on her. That was very important to me. I knew where she lived and I made a beeline to her house hoping that I would find her there. "He went out with another girl last night", she said. "He took her to the Playhouse. I ain't having no black nigger of mine dating any other nigger but me."

I told her that I would have to turn her in but I would much rather have her tell the police that she was the one who had done it. I tried to impress on her that she might get a lighter sentence. She really did not care that they knew she had done it. It served him right for messing around with somebody else and she was glad that she had hurt him. We went to the police station together and she told them all of the facts. It is all right, Ms. Jones, do not worry about me. I got what I wanted. The boy did not press charges. She was suspended from school for carrying a concealed weapon for the rest of the year. Can you imagine, they got back together and I saw them holding hands downtown not long after the incident. The boy said that he felt all warm inside knowing that she cared that much for him. He also turned out to be a hero among his friends. Wonders never cease! It was not long before she was pregnant, by him, I think. You never know.

There was another boy in that homeroom that I will call James. He was pretty tough too. I always felt as though he was on drugs but never knew for sure. One morning I was calling the role and he didn't answer. Some of the kids said that he had been killed over the weekend. I thought that they were joking, little did I know. Dead he was. It came out in the local paper that his body was found behind the old school that had been deserted when integration had occurred. Shot in the head twice. The paper said the police felt like it was a drug deal gone bad. I liked James. He had starting working real hard and I felt like he wanted to graduate in the worst way. He said that he would be the first one in his family to finish high school and they had all gotten together to chip in money to buy his graduation invitations. He had bought fifteen invitations. Now what was I going to do with those when they came in? They were already paid for. I went to the funeral. It wasn't until about a week later. Do you know why the blacks hold such a long wake? They are collecting money. The funeral homes will not bury them until the bill is paid.

If you have never been to a black funeral, you haven't lived. Preferably, one in which you are the only white. You will know then how integration feels to the minority person, only twice as bad. The success during those years at someone's funeral usually depended on how many whites came. Every black funeral had black nurses standing around to give out smelling salts to the people who fainted. They were all dressed in white with little hats just like the nurses wear. This was true in our location; I can't speak for anywhere else. Using this as a benchmark, James's funeral was not much of a success. I was the only white there. Poor James! He probably got a little taste of the money you can make when you sell drugs. He never had any, and once he got to taking them himself, he was hooked by the big boys. Whatever they wanted, he had to do. Maybe he was skimming off the top or maybe he didn't turn enough money in for the amount of drugs he was supposed to sell. He never could add very well.

Don't you feel the pain in all of this? The hopelessness of the black community. They were relegated to the most menial jobs around, like janitorial work or digging ditches. There were no good jobs for the blacks. Had I been black at that time, I would have been the most belligerent person around? I would have been mad at the world and yes, I would have thought that the whites owed me something and anything that I could screw out of them was mine. They lived in houses that I wouldn't let my dog live in. The owners charged awful rates and they never fixed them up. Most of them did not even have indoor plumbing. Three or four black families lived in two rooms together. Sometimes there were as many as ten people in two rooms. I would have been on welfare too and yes, I would have played the system just like they did. I would be on welfare and work too, and never tell the government. What a mess!!!

Not all blacks lived this way, not all blacks were this way. I had quite a few blacks every year that came from educated, above middle class families. Most of their parents were teachers, dentists, or doctors. They still harbored the same feeling of low self-esteem. They felt that they did not belong anywhere. Their parents made them do their work and this was unacceptable by their own race. It was not cool to succeed. The blacks did not accept them, and the whites certainly did not associate with them. They were in no man's land. It was easy to get them into the better universities but many of their parents wanted them to go to the black school where the parents had graduated. Now that was a mess. Here was me saying one thing, the parent saying another and the student wanting something else. Back in those days, directive counseling was a must in some situations and I practiced it regularly. Now you answer me this. If you have a real smart black student who could be accepted anywhere in the country and they ask you where it would be best for them to go. Would you say Podunck Black University where you knew that zero nursing students passed the state boards in nursing and where zero pre-law students got into law school? I don't think so!

Finding a job after graduation had to be considered also. Now all of us know that the best way you get a job is family connections. Right? Well the blacks didn't have many family connections where the friend ran a business. If you are a job recruiter and had the choice of a black student who attended a prestigious white college and one who attended Podunck Black University, which one would you pick?

When I was sitting for my oral dissertation, the professors asked me what my impression of the blacks was and how I thought they would react to integration. Do you know what my answer was? I said that I thought they were free spirits. 'Marching to their own drum' was the only way that they could survive. We would never be able to corral them with the white folk's rules, or subjugate them to the white folk's ways and that's what we were trying to do. All we could ever have would be bedlam. They all thought that I was brilliant. You know how it is when you are sitting in ivory towers, the front line is where the action is and they had never seen it. It probably saved my life and got me my degree and I am thankful for that. Although at the time, I never thought that what I felt was any different from what everybody else knew too.

They had a great big Ku Klux Klan sign up as you came into our town, I mean big. It said something about they were protecting our community. It had a big finger on it pointing right at the car as you drove by. This was around 1969, and every time I looked at it, I wanted to cry. They marched with their sheets every now and then and I was always surprised that one of them wasn't killed. I guess everyone was too afraid. My black students told me that when they ate in a restaurant, someone would walk by and leave them a little card that said, "The Ku Klux Klan is watching you". It scared them to death. How would you feel? It would make me so mad that I would want to clean house, send them all off to somewhere else. I know that this was true because the students brought me the cards to see. The members of the Klan were not someone out in the back woods. They were the man that fixed my car, the mayor, the restaurant owner, the cab driver, a member of the board of education, your next- door neighbor, a lawyer, anybody. I think our little community might have been one of the last strongholds for the Klan in our state. It didn't help integration, knowing that they were always there watching.

The thing that saved us was the responsible blacks in our community and the blacks in education. They knew that we had to survive together or lose it all. They talked in their churches, their communities, their activity halls, and some of us went with them, some of us who really cared. We pleaded for their support, for their involvement for them to exert their influence on their children for their help, and we got it. They gave up the education of their children to the white man and they got shortchanged.

The Klan took one of our students one night. I know this sounds like something out of a science fiction book but they took him from one of the local black hangouts and carried him to the woods. They all had on their sheets and everything. It seemed that he was seeing one of the white girls in our school and they wanted to impress on him that it was a no-no. Much later, it was not a no-no and the black senior boys preyed on the white freshman girls because it was macho and "screw the white man", they said. What better way to get back at him for all that he had done than through the children. This was not a conscious thought but I felt that it was there. The Klan got away with it and they brought him back to school the next morning without even taking him home. He was so scared that I am not sure that he ever got over it. They told him that if he ever told what happened to him that they would kill him. I know for a fact that they would have too and no one would have ever suffered the consequences. Needless to say, he never talked to the white girl again. When he and I were talking in my office that day that they brought him back, it was almost like he felt he deserved it. He hated white people but it was as if he knew that he was overstepping the boundaries that were set for him by society. He felt that he needed punishing. He was also one of my homeroom students. Are you getting the picture about my homeroom?

I have seen this boy, now almost thirty years later, on the streets. He has children of his own. We always stop and talk about old times but he never mentions his experience with the Klan and I don't either. They are no longer in evidence and no one ever hears of them now. Times have changed and the fear of them is gone.

I know that my principal thought he was breaking me in right when he gave me that homeroom, but in reality, he was doing me the biggest favor of all time. The guidance department earned the name of being there to help students. Somehow, students felt that the guidance department called you when you were in trouble. The counselors tried to make you see the error of your ways and sent you back to class. I don't know where they got that idea, maybe from middle school experiences, but it was so far from what we tried to do that it made me sick when I heard them say it. The word spread from my homeroom, I am sure, that the new white woman was o.k. You have to make inroads and sometimes it takes a long time and sometimes things just fall into your lap.

I lost three boys from my homeroom that first year not counting the one that got killed. They were suspended permanently, one for selling dope, one for bringing a gun on campus, and one for fighting. The fighting boy would have been a ten-day suspension but the idiot pulled a knife. Three or four of the students failed because they were absent too many days and one of the girls had her baby too near the end of school to make her work up. About twelve of them just plain failed one of the courses they were taking. Do you know what that meant? Half of the class graduated and if that isn't success, I don't know what is. Oh, you should have seen their families at graduation. I have never seen anyone so proud. I smiled for more pictures in that one day than I have ever had taken in my whole life. The homeroom teachers got to call the names of their homeroom students out at the podium on graduation day. They were probably the only ones who knew how to pronounce the names. Almost every kid kissed me on the cheek when they shook my hand. I have never forgotten it. I was as proud as they were. The whooping and hollering that went on as each kid crossed the stage was deafening but I knew where it was coming from and it was music to my ears for the family and the kid. After it was over, everyone was upset over the lack of respect the audience had for the ceremony and what in the world could the school do to put an end to it. I just smiled to myself because I knew that it showed how little they knew about a culture different from their own.

They are still doing it thirty years later at graduation ceremonies and I honestly believe they will always do it. It's a part of the free spirit. Just like how they get involved in church ceremonies, clapping and all and singing out. How they can all dance and move with all that freedom and the whites are so inhibited! We are afraid that someone will make fun of us. You know we are not as free as they are and they think that it is the other way around.

CHAPTER 8

Group Guidance

That is enough about my homeroom for now. I am tired of talking about it. Let's move on to my 'group guidance'. Back in those days, you had to have classroom guidance once a week. You set it up with some teacher and you would go in their room and do some kind of occupational thing or motivational thing or attitude adjustment thing. Boy, teachers hated it and I did too. They felt like you were taking up their class time for junk and they didn't mind telling you so. It always worked better for me not to do it on a routine basis and to rotate your teachers so that you only hit the same one once a month. That made it a little better to swallow. We also had to do small group counseling and I loved that.

The first class that I set up was with six black girls to talk about sex. The health department wanted me to do this because so many girls were getting pregnant out of wedlock and were not taking care of the babies with regular doctor visits and they thought that they would come to some of the group sessions and push regular doctor visits and talk about the services that the health department offered. There were complications of pregnancy, labor, or delivery and congenital birth defects. Infant mortality rates were running 30% higher among teenagers than for mothers over the age of twenty. It was estimated during those years, that if the current trends continued, four out of every ten teenage girls would have at least one pregnancy while in their teens. Studies revealed that up to 80% of the nation's four million sexually active teenagers failed to use birth control, due largely to ignorance about methods or about the availability of contraceptive devices. I learned more about sex in those sessions than I had ever learned in my thirty-nine years prior to that. I started off, on a scale of one to ten, about ten notches above where they were. Little did I know, they didn't even know how they got pregnant or what kept them from it. Don't laugh!

Once that first group got to going good and they got over their initial reservations about each other and me and we got over the trust thing and the meeting each other thing; well, as the kids would say the "shit hit the fan". Remember earlier in the book I told you about my group guidance sessions. I started the session somewhere up there with the biological thing and the pictures and all and the hormones and all of that kind of thing. Well Donna, let's call her Donna because I have forgotten her name, said "Now Ms. Jones, all of us know how you keep from getting pregnant. Let's start from there. My Grandmother always told me that if you plaited your hair real tight, almost so tight that you couldn't smile, you could never get pregnant." You don't believe me? I will swear on a stack of bibles that is exactly what she said. The most amazing thing was that no one disputed her words.

Then one of the other girls said, "I'll tell you something else that works. My Grandmother told me that if you did it standing up you could never get pregnant." At least this sounded a little more plausible than plaiting your hair tight.

My generation didn't know anything about sex either. Our mothers certainly were not going to tell us; they were Southern Victorian ladies and sex was never brought up in polite conversation. We certainly never read anything about it because we were too embarrassed to buy the books; and the pictures, heaven forbid. We never even knew about 'periods' except from each other when they started. We just knew that they were something we had to do and if you didn't have one you were pregnant. I am not sure that we knew at that age that a man was involved. We learned that later. Of course, if we had older brothers or sisters sometimes they told us a little more. Here I was talking about scientific sex to six girls who were never going to believe what I said anyway. Their grandmothers took precedence and besides, I was white.

When you stand up in front of a large group and talk to young people, you never know where they are coming from, what they understand, or whether you are talking so far above their heads, they will never catch up. They are too intimidated by their peers to speak out, so you never know. In a small group, you know and I knew right then that I had my work cut out for me. I would lie awake at night trying to come up with some way that I could penetrate the veil of ignorance that surrounded them. I am not sure that I ever learned, but maybe somewhere, something that I said made a difference to someone. All you need is a few successes and that will keep you going for a long time.

I ran many group sessions on sex after that, even wrote some up and published them, but I never really felt that I knew any answers. I even got the feeling sometimes that I was not the group leader even though I was supposed to be. It was almost like I stepped out of reality and was dream-walking among these strange people who all knew what the other one was talking about and the dialogue flowed around me. It consumed me sometimes. They all felt that I was wonderful. Little did they know that 'the wonderful' was my ability to listen. I often wished that I could teach parents how to listen but it is much harder to live with listening to teenage-land than to visit there. I used to teach the course that people who worked in 'Contact' took. Contact was the telephone system that the churches sponsored where you could call in without divulging who you were and receive help for any problem that you might have. I spent three sessions teaching about listening, how to, when to, why. I found wonderful tapes on it and good videos, so there are places that you can go to learn. However, there are some people who could never learn. You know some of them I am sure.

A child in trouble will turn to anybody for help. They will ask teachers, counselors, Contact, ministers, mental health, anybody until they find the one who gives them an answer that they feel is right for them. Then, all of the helping agencies in the community would meet and discuss some of our hardest cases; we did that once a month for many years.

These meetings would all have the same people. Even though we did not divulge names, we could tell. I always hoped that no one was giving out pat answers to young people, when they did not know the situation. So many people talk from their own background without taking into consideration where the other person is coming from. It's so hard to walk on both sides of the fence or see both sides of the picture. I think that it is a gift or a curse, whichever you would like to call it.

Before I leave this sex and pregnancy stuff, there is one more thing that I have to tell you. I would set up meetings for Social Services and the health department with the girls in high school that were already pregnant, and there were a lot of them. They could explain to the students the services that they offered. I never knew a black student who would have an abortion. You could explain all of their options until you were blue in the face and go over each one very carefully with them without showing any kind of partiality about any of them but you were wasting your time. The white girls would elect abortion every time and all they had to find was the money to do it. So, most of these girls that Social Services met with were black.

When I listened to the health nurse explain all of the services that were available to them, it almost made me want to be pregnant. There was free everything, physicals, immunizations, pediatric screenings, prenatal care, pregnancy testing, counseling, breast exams, day care, baby food, milk, body composition analysis (whatever that was), birth control methods and free contraceptives. All of that was available 30 years ago. I was talking with someone in the health department not long ago who said that they had a new grant to provide counseling to girls who came in for pregnancy testing so that maybe they would not be back the second time. Well, they had that 30 years ago too. They even have an Adolescent Parenting Program set up where you have a volunteer to work with these girls who feel that they are having trouble with parenting skills and are not functioning appropriately as a parent. I needed one of those people in my life. Anyway, I began to feel that the tail was wagging the dog instead of the dog waging the tail. It seemed to me that the emphasis was being placed on the end result rather than the beginning. They are still doing it thirty years later.

CHAPTER 9

Odds and Ends

I know that after all of this heavy reading, you need a little levity so we will go back to the witch of a counselor that shared the guidance department with me. Damn her! I saw her the other day at the nursing home, she must be 100, and all of those years with her flooded my memory. She was a patient, not visiting like me, at the nursing home I mean. Well, to go on, it was part of my senior responsibilities to administer the SAT, also dispensing all of the information to the students about when it was to be given, when it was time to sign up and all of that stuff. The Testing Service would notify us and send all of the stuff through the mail in plenty of time to get it to the students. She would hide it from me. That's right; hide it from me. She wanted me to fall flat of my face that first year so that she could have her job back. Don't make me mad, I can fight with the best of them.

I went to war with her. I really did some rotten things but I will not tell you about them, only the half rotten things. I would get the janitor to let me into her office at least once a week on some pretense or other that he always believed, or said he did since he liked me. I would riffle through all of her things until I found something that pertained to me and I would take it. She knew that I was doing it but she couldn't complain because it was mine to begin with. That damn secretary was conspiring with her anyway, and she would show her all of my letters and things that I would send out and forward my incoming phone calls to her first when she thought they were important. There was nothing that I did that the witch didn't know about. Now can you imagine grown women acting like that? Part of it stopped when the secretary ran out in front of a car one night and got killed. We did without one the rest of the year and that worked out better for me. I never was a good typist but I sure learned to be one that year.

In faculty meetings, Elma would always have these cutting remarks to make like, "Ask Ms. Jones. She knows everything or thinks she does". Or, "Just give her a little time and she will have that in her office too; better hide it if you want to keep it". She never read '*How to Win Friends and Influence People*', that's for sure. Honey dripped from my mouth whenever someone else was around and I talked to her but when the two of us were alone, boy the words I could say to her! I was as bitchy as she was. She only lasted for that first year and then she asked for a transfer to one of the other schools in the county where she could be senior counselor. They let her go at mid-year, they couldn't stand her either.

The thing that I wanted to tell you next keeps running around in my head but for some reason the sprockets will not click in to run the reel. That's what happens when you get old. Maybe the sprockets wear out. Anyway, do you know what 'male chauvinist pigs' are? The dictionary defines it as 'unusual devotion to ones male race.' I define it as men who look down on women and talk themselves into believing that women are inferior. The world used to be full of them but most of them have gotten so old now and they know that women have to look after them and they have mellowed. Back in the sixties, the world was full of them and women, bless their hearts, learned to get along with them by making them think that all of the ideas were theirs. They smiled and acted dumb and 'honey this' and 'honey that' and acted coy and sweet. Well, it was what worked. I spent my whole life making men think that I was the proverbial dumb blonde, and I usually got what I wanted. I don't really think that most men thought girls were inferior. I think that it was an ego thing with them and they played the game.

Now back to what I was going to tell you before I got sidetracked. My principal came down one day and said that every morning he wanted me to stand in the hall and look for girls when they came in who had no bra on. Honest to goodness this is true. I was to take them to one of the principals and they would call their parents to come and get them. The contention was that the lack of that article kept the boys from learning and keeping their minds on the subject matter. I tried to tell him that it was not good exposure for a guidance counselor because we were supposed to be there for the student and not as a disciplinarian, but it was to no avail. It didn't take me long to learn that most of the girls who came to school with no bra on, took it off after they left home and it was stuffed in their pocketbook. All I ended up having to do was smile, cock my head and nod toward the principal's office. They knew they had been caught and would make a beeline to the bathroom to put the bra on. A couple of times I came to school without one but nobody noticed. The administration kept changing where I stood so it wasn't long before most of the girls arrived with the proper attire. I formed the opinion that the whole male administration was just lecherous old men.

We had this table in the hall at the front door where the students came in. The seniors, who were absent the day before, had to take their note for being absent to this oaf of a man teacher who was about 23 and was so sarcastic that the sarcasm dripped from his mouth like spittle. Granted, most of the seniors wrote their own notes, but most of them could write. Their parents couldn't.

He would read the note out loud to be cute; then he would say things like, "Oh, I see your period was so bad that you had to go to bed. What did you do, lay out to screw your boyfriend all day? I noticed on the absentee list he was absent too."

Alternately, "This says that you went to the clinic. Did you have to have a pregnancy test?" He thought he was so cute. Well, after he finished with the students they would be in my office crying because he had embarrassed them so badly in front of their peers. It made me so mad. When I would see him at teachers meetings or in the hall, I would tell him to stop embarrassing the students. Nothing seemed to faze him and on and on it went.

One morning he was especially rude and sarcastic. He told one girl out loud, after he had read her note saying she was sick, "Well I saw you at the abortion clinic yesterday as you went in, so I guess you were sick if you had that done."

It burnt me up. I went flying out there, got right in his face and told him if he didn't stop, I was going to beat him up personally. He stood up with his mouth right in my face and made some comment about "you and who else". Now remember there were probably 100 students waiting in line to get their notes signed. I hit him so hard with a left hook (I am left handed, and he wasn't expecting that from me) that it knocked him down on the floor on his butt. I can still see the expression on his face when he looked up at me. I guess he could have taken me to court on assault and battery charges but cooler heads prevailed. He got the point and he toned his comments down a little but he didn't stop completely. He wasn't back the next year either. I'm sorry. A person can take just so much and back then, I was a hot head as I have already told you.

There were a lot of students lost during the late sixties and early seventies. They would carry signs in the halls, protesting against this and that. They wore long black greatcoats. They had long hair and were experimenting with a few drugs. They were sensitive, eager to save the world and mad with their parents and society in general. The Vietnam War was in full swing. The draft board was working overtime. There were campus protests on every campus in the United States. Four students were killed at Kent State in Ohio by National Guardsmen who were called out to preserve order on the campus. Students at Jackson State in Mississippi were also shot and killed for political reasons. The protesting carried over to our high school campus.

One day this handsome young senior came into my office, closed the door and sat down opposite me. "You have to help me. The draft board has informed me that I have to talk to you about becoming a conscientious objector and you have to certify me as one." First I ever heard of that! He gave me some stuff that they had sent to me and after two weeks with this sensitive, intelligent boy who was becoming a man, I certified him as a conscientious objector. I was never really sure that he was. How could anybody be? I did know that I would not have wanted him to cover my back in a battle, nor would I have wanted him to be a part of a team with a battle objective.

I have seen him many times since those sessions. He went on to become a surgeon, one of the most famous brain surgeons on the East Coast. Not long ago, I heard that he had chucked it all, wife, children, surgery and had gone to the West to make pottery. He was lost, lost like his best friend who had gone to Alaska after high school to fish for salmon. Actually, his friend was running from the draft. He returned to become a dentist, and gave it all up to go back to Alaska. Lost like another friend who graduated first in his class and had retreated into a Walden-type woods and formed a commune. What a horrible time for young people to have grown up! They were damned if they did and dammed if they didn't.

A father came to see his son during this time. The son had not been home for three days and the father heard that he was in school. He came in my office and asked me to get the boy for him. I went up but the boy refused to come down and talk to the father. It was one of the most prestigious families in our town and I saw them all of the time socially. I have never hated anything as badly as I hated to tell that father that his son did not want to talk to him. He came down to talk to me after school was out and apologized for putting me in the middle. He said that his father had never understood him, never tried to, and he was never home. His father had no respect for him and he was never going back. He didn't, and I never saw him again after that day. Neither did his parents.

A student who graduated first in his class during that time went to Alaska and worked on a boat fishing for Salmon. He never returned and never went to college. I heard many years later that he had married and lived in Alaska. His parents had never seen him since the day that he graduated.

I knew the parents of these boys. They were good people. They worked hard for their children and wanted them to have the very best. They went to church, were scout leaders, volunteers in the school, joined the PTA, and basically did everything that made the students grow up well adjusted and motivated.

Another senior came into my office during those years and pleaded with me to go and talk to his parents about sending him to a drug treatment program. He said he had told his mother that he needed to go but she was afraid to tell his father. His father was a very volatile man and the student was afraid of him. For that matter, so was the mother. He was an only child and the father thought that he was the most wonderful thing since sliced bread. I hated so badly to get in the middle of that catfight but I cared so much for the boy and I felt that if he wanted saving, the least that I could do was help him. I had dated his father in high school and I think that both of the parents respected me so I took a big deep breath and waded in. The water was almost too deep for me. I called and asked if I could come over one night and talk to them. I just out and out told them that their son was involved in drugs and he needed help. The father started screaming and yelling abusive words at me and I sat and took them until the worst of his anger was vented. He was still fuming when I got up and left. I knew that I would never be friends with them again. I had crossed the line. About a week later, the student was gone and about a week after that, I received a call from his counselor at the treatment center where he was. He was with the counselor and he put him on the phone to talk with me. I have never been thanked so royally for anything in my life, nor have I ever felt better about anything that I did.

There is no silver lining, I never saw his parents socially again. Neither one of them ever spoke to me again.

I did see the boy though. He was happily married and had three children. He looked wonderful, his wife was beautiful and he seemed so proud of his children. I did not talk to him about high school, but from what he said, I gathered that he was very successful. He made it too!

I am amazed at how often 'Lerrner's Hill' can be climbed from such unpromising circumstances.

I never could understand why people wanted to be senior counselor, but it was coveted by all the guidance counselors that I ever met. It was like the pinnacle of counseling. It is a lot more work than any other position that a counselor could hold and the responsibilities are furious if you are serious about your job. Imagine the responsibility of helping young people decide what they want to be when they have just starting thinking about it seriously for the first time in their life. It means helping them decide where the best school would be for them, helping them decide whether they even want to go or not, finding the finances so that they can, being sure that they all are taking what they need to graduate. I don't care what anybody tells you about group guidance, you absolutely have to talk with every senior individually at least twice that senior year to help them, encourage them, motivate them and do whatever it takes to prepare them for that next big step in their life. This applies particularly to the black race. They have low self-esteem and it is very difficult for them to feel that they can have any successes in college.

If the truth were known, I feel that every counselor at every grade level should have those individual sessions with students starting in the ninth grade. I know it's hard and time-consuming but it's a must. I guess the best way possible for a counselor to be effective would be for them to move up as the students move up. This would mean that you would know your students better and really be able to serve them better. There are disadvantages to this method like the changing college scene, knowing all of the scholarships, knowing the admissions procedures. Being on a first name basis with admissions directors helps a student so much. If you are not the kind of counselor that calls all the time, you can be the deciding factor for a marginal student. I have seen many, many students who would not have been accepted except for the personal touch that was given for them.

CHAPTER 10

From Humble Prospects

While I am on this subject, it would be a good time to tell you that you can never tell what a student might be capable of doing. Don't ever sell one short. They could have taken five years in high school in the lowest classes available and still be a shining success in college. Your job is to encourage, encourage and encourage. Let me tell you a story that is the best illustration of this that I know. I was very fortunate to have this happen to me very early in my career.

I had a very sweet little senior one day in my office whose name we will say was Betty. She had been identified as a Learning Disabled student and had been in LD classes all of twelve years in school. I think that I found out later that she had repeated the first grade. You know how the school system likes to put labels on children and how they like to use all of those letters like LD, EMH, ADHD, AG, IQ, PDC, IEP, they go on and on. Anyway, Betty said, "You know, I would love to go and get some more education. I want a really good job when I graduate." Bells went off in my head. What was I going to say to this precious child? Of course,

"I think that would be wonderful" is what came out of my mouth". We talked about all kinds of avenues for her but it turned out that she did not want to go to the local Community College because of the stigma that was attached to it at that time. She wanted to get away from home. Most of them did, because it was glamorous. Her parents were fairly well to do and she had an older brother who had just graduated from college. After two or three days of going around and around, she decided on a two-year college that offered a secretarial degree. I will honestly say here that I did not think that she would succeed but I did not tell her that.

She graduated from high school and took off to the secretarial school. It was about a year later that she came back to see me and told me that after she arrived at school, she decided to enter the two-year college transfer program instead of taking the secretarial degree. She said that she was taking only remedial courses now but she was doing very well in them. I was a little surprised but I knew that this meant she was really taking high school courses over again. The thing that surprised me was that she had not even been in regular high school courses when she was in high school but rather a watered down version with lots of individual help. Well the next time that I saw her, she had graduated from her two-year school and had been acceptance to a very prestigious state university as a second semester sophomore. This meant that most of her courses had transferred, which in turn meant her course grades were a C or better. This really surprised me. The next thing that I heard she had graduated magna cum laud with a four year business degree. I nearly fainted. That's not the end of the story. Four years later, she came back to the high school with her Ph.D. to thank me for encouraging her to go and find herself. She had graduated with a 4.0 from graduate school. I know that this must sound like something that I made up but this wonderful woman still lives in my hometown. I still see her often, and if you wish, we could go and talk to her together. I am sure that she would tell you the story herself.

I feel sure that there are many, many mothers out there who could find solace when reading about Betty. Don't ever give up on your children. Lead them, but don't push too hard, love them but give them space and help them over That Hill. You may be very surprised at the adult that emerges.

I never did understand how my girls learned to cook and clean. They certainly didn't learn it from me. They never watched me. They never asked about a reciepe and they never cleaned their rooms. One of them even told her friends, in my presence by the way, that all she ever had for breakfast was a pop tart but when, she promised, she had children she would fix them a good breakfast every morning to start the day off right. She failed to mention that it was all that I could do to get her to eat at all. It tickles me to watch her family now. Even her husband eats only pop tarts for breakfast.

CHAPTER 11

Teachers, Students, and Sex

I haven't touched on the teacher-student problem that every school has. I don't mean the discipline problem but the sexual problem. Well, we had more than our share of those but the one that stands out most in my mind sounds like something that Stephen King would write about.

We had this history teacher that was probably one of the most handsome men I had ever seen. He was tall, dark, and dark headed and when you talked to him, he would lean toward you and look straight in your eyes as though he was devouring every word that you said. Well, needless to say, all of the students loved him and the girls loved him literally. He always wore a small gold cross in his lapel button and this really turned me on because I thought it was such a nice statement to make when a teacher works with young people. Let them know where you stand.

One day he came into my office and said that one of the teachers had told him that I might be able to help him with his problem. It turned out that one of the junior girls had been visiting him almost every day after school in his classroom and she had told him that she had a crush on him. She had said that she couldn't live without him and so on, and so on. I don't know whether you call it a 'crush' or not, but we did then. He told me her name and it turned out that she lived in my neighborhood. I promised him that I would call her in and talk to her and maybe we could nip her feelings of romance in the bud before it got too bad. Really, his job was at stake if he were accused of having a relationship with her.

Her side of the story was not quite like his when she was telling me all about what had transpired between them but this did not surprise me too much. She said that her parents knew all about it and they did not have a problem with her seeing him. I asked her if the two of them had ever been out on a date. She said not a real date but that they had been alone together at night quite a few times and that he had professed his love for her. I explained to her that if anyone found out about it, he would lose his job and I also told her that he had talked to me about the relationship. It was near the end of the school year and I knew that the summer would cool things off a little because they would not have the opportunity to see each other as much. I thought one time that she might be lying to me about her parents knowing, but I did not pursue it with them. I kept my eyes open and would walk by his room after school but I did not see her in there and I had heard nothing from the 'grapevine' that would indicate there was something going on.

He came down to see me about two weeks after I talked to her and he said that things had cooled off and he thanked me for helping him. There were still things that puzzled me about the whole situation, but I didn't have time to dwell on them and I went on with the rest of the millions of things that I had to do.

It was about a month later that one of the sophomore girls in the school committed suicide. She was an honor student, beautiful, well liked and came from a wonderful family. The whole school went into mourning. No one could understand why. She had gone out into a workroom that was near her house and shot herself in the mouth with a shotgun. I think all 1500 students in our school attended her funeral and most of the teachers. She had left a note and asked her parent's forgiveness but it was very nonspecific and left no clue as to why she might have done it.

This was told to me, I did not read her note. Our crisis team spent many hours with the students, after her death, trying to help them deal with their loss.

About a week after the funeral, it turned out that the tall good-looking history teacher had received a number of essays from her that indicated that she was very depressed. The students had seen her turn them in and asked to read them and naturally, I heard about it. The word on the street (the students' street) was that they had been having an affair, unproven of course, and the handsome history teacher had broken it off. You know that my mind went back to the other episode when I heard about it and I began to wonder. I put it out of my mind; after all, he did wear a cross.

About a week before school was out, one of my seniors came in to talk with me about a personal problem she was having with her history teacher. It was him. She said that she was in love with him and she wanted to marry him. She knew that she had to wait until school was out because he would lose his job if anyone found out and she didn't want that to happen. I know that my mouth fell open when she told me. I tried so hard to keep a straight face but it was impossible. I explained to her that once she graduated, there would be no problem because she would not be a student in the school and he would be able to date her openly.

The student went away to school after that year, a private school, very close, for her senior year. He left and went north to a private junior college to teach. I never knew whether or not he was asked to leave or if he just wanted a better job. He was a wonderful teacher. About two months after he left, one of his students from our school went up to visit him for the weekend. She had graduated the year before and was away at college. I read in the paper about her death while she was there They had gone boating on a lake close to his new school and the boat had turned over and she had drowned. He wore a cross in his buttonhole.

Every year we had at least two or three cases that involved romantic relationships between teachers and students. In every situation that I got involved in, I could see that the student had been as much at fault as the teacher. Now I know that the teacher is supposed to be more mature, disciplined, and better able to handle the situation but in most of these cases it was usually a young first-year male teacher and a senior girl. That male ego is something to behold. What havoc the whole affair could bring before it was all over.

Sometimes the students got pregnant, sometimes the male teachers were married and the wife was involved. Sometimes the parents of the student got involved. Always it ended up with so many people hurt and sometime there was nothing that you could do to stop it. It had to run its course.

One case in particular really got to me because it involved the daughter of a friend. This beautiful black girl started having a relationship with the tennis coach and it was very hard for me to be objective about the whole thing because he was married and I knew that it could only end up hurting everyone. She was beautiful and probably started the whole thing by flirting with him. Then it got too hot for her to handle.

I must admit that I walked into a trap myself once. I pulled a muscle in my leg playing basketball for the faculty and I could hardly walk on it. I was really in bad shape. One of the football players told me that it would feel much better if I got in the whirlpool every day for a while and relaxed it. I didn't even know where the whirlpool was so he offered to take me there and show me how to use it the first time I went. This sounds very "up front" doesn't it.

Well, he and I went out to the field house, away from the school but on school grounds, and when I saw the whirlpool, I knew that I was in trouble. It was raised up from the ground and you really had to get into the thing to get your leg in. I really never thought about it being constructed like that. I kind'a tucked up my dress to put my leg down in the water and he turned the whirlpool on. He busied himself on the other side of the room, and I had to pull my dress up a little farther when the water started swirling. The funniest feeling crept over me and I knew that the boy felt something also from the way that he was looking. I told him to turn the water off and he did. He said that I had not been in long enough to do any good. I looked very straight at him and said that I was sorry that I had put him in that position and it would not happen again. I also told him that I was stupid and I did not visualize the set up. I never went back but every time that I saw that boy, I had the funniest feeling. It could have very easily developed into something and for all that I know the boy thought that I was interested in him and was just leading him on.

Counselors learn in school that you should refer students to public and private agencies and practitioners outside of the school system who can meet the student's needs on a long-term basis. It doesn't work that way except in very extreme cases. Then, the student is schizophrenic or manic-depressive or has some serious chemical imbalance. Generally speaking, you have to do the best that you can with what is handed you each day and not let yourself end up doing only crisis counseling. You have to keep the big picture in mind and remember that preventive counseling is what it really is about.

CHAPTER 12

In a Family Way

This whole book could be about all of the girls who came to me who were pregnant and all of the different avenues that they took, how the pregnancy affected their life, the boys' life and the life of their parents. I will only talk about a few here because there are other issues that need to be addressed.

There were many different ways that I heard about pregnancy. Teachers would ask the student to come and talk with me if they suspected it. I would see the student in the hall and suspect it. Parents would call me and ask me to find out if they suspected it and last but not least, the student would come to me herself because she was so frightened.

The first thing that I noticed when Marsha came into my office was that she was very overweight. She had pretty red hair and a radiant smile but I could tell by her eyes that she was troubled. I knew that finding out what the real problem was would be difficult, so becoming familiar with each other would have to come first.

"I am on the Academic Super Bowl Team and I love it," she said. "They picked thirteen students out of about fifty and I was one of them." I knew about the Academic Super Bowl Team. All of the schools all over the United States had a team and they competed with each other on a local level, a regional level, a state level and on a national level. It was really quite an honor to be picked to play on one but it was very time consuming. The team practiced every day and usually competed about once a month with other teams. The game was played by an announcer calling out a question and each student had a bell in front of them and the one who rang their bell first and knew the right answer got some points, something like that. You had to think very fast, be smart and quick with your hands. I figured out right away that Marsha was an honor student and probably headed for college. I was a little confused about her family background because her clothes did not indicate that her family was middle class or above, maybe the problem was family related. I began to ask her about her family. Every question had an answer from her that returned us to the Super Bowl Team.

As an example, "Do you drive a car to school?"

"No, I do not have a car. I have to ride with friends to the Super Bowl Games. Every now and then my father will take me."

"Do both your Mother and Father work?" I asked.

"Yes, and that's why it's so difficult for me to get home after Super Bowl practice."

"Do you have a job?"

"No, if I did I would not be able to be on the Super Bowl Team," she said. On and on it went, just like that. I was trying so hard to ask the right question. She was fidgeting and nervous and I knew that soon I would lose her and I would not have been any help. Our conversation had gone on for about an hour by this time.

Right out of the blue she said, "You know I have never had a date. I have never been off in a car with a boy. Mother and Daddy will not let me date."

This was loaded statement. I was fishing so deep for the right question that my brain hurt. "Have you dated without telling them?" I asked.

"Oh no!" she said. "I would never do that. The only time that I have ever been with a boy was after a Super Bowl match at a near-by High School and I think that I got pregnant then and I don't know what to do. I don't even know the boys name."

I almost fell out of my chair! How could any boy have talked this beautiful child into having intercourse with him when she had never even been in a car with a boy before? There was my middle-class background showing again. Of course, there was another side of the coin. There was a possibility that what she was saying was not really true? Everything went through my mind. Perhaps her father had abused her sexually. Perhaps a relative had his way with her. Perhaps a sibling!

After about a week of talking together, I finally convinced her that this problem was not going away and she needed to tell her parents. I offered to meet with the three of them in my office if she needed my support but I did tell her that I felt that it was best if she told them on her own. They might be embarrassed if they found out that someone knew before they had the opportunity to hear it. I also explained to her that the boy should be held accountable and should help bear some of the financial burdens that would occur. I told her that it would be easy for me to find out who the boy was. She never came to talk with me after that visit. She had told me that she thought that she was about five months pregnant. You could not tell that she was pregnant by looking at her and it was May at the time we had our first conversation.

I saw her in the hall at the beginning of the next school year and she told me that she wanted me to see her baby, she seemed so proud of it, and that she would bring it to school one day when the students were out. About a month later I was in Wall-Mart and she was there with her mother and the baby. She had evidently told her mother about our conversations because her mother thanked me for helping her. The baby was a boy, it was precious and it was black. You could tell that the grandmother loved it very much. Her face lit up every time she spoke of all of the things that the baby could do. Aren't babies wonderful! They bridge so many gaps and mend so many fences without even being able to say a word.

One of the strangest stories along this line was the time that a teacher came to me and said that she thought one of her students might be pregnant and would I please talk to her. I would swear to you on a stack of Bibles that when that child walked into my office, I was not real sure that she was pregnant. She sat down and we talked and talked and talked some more. We slid around the issue and skirted the issue and I kept thinking that she would tell me. Finally, I just blurted it out and asked her and she denied it. Now there is not much you can do when a student just right out denies something.

She went home that night and delivered an eight-pound baby. Neither of her parents knew that she was pregnant and somehow they blamed the school for not letting them know. Even though I was not sure, it is hard for me to believe that I could have lived with that child for the nine months of her pregnancy and not know that she was pregnant.

CHAPTER 13

The Faculty

There is so much that I want to tell you that it is hard to know where to go from here. Perhaps you need to digest what you have heard about the students for a while so I will turn to the faculty and some of my relationships with them.

The principal found out that I could write a pretty good reference letter so he decided that I would write all of his and let him sign his name to them. We had gotten on pretty good terms by this time and I agreed because I felt that the students would benefit more from my writing them than if he did. He was pretty blunt and to the point. It could be the difference in a student receiving a scholarship or not. In addition, I knew that he would owe me. You know, if a student needed a favor it might be easier for me to talk him into it because I was helping him. It came easy to me to write those letters anyway so that was the deal.

The school was big, 1500-plus students. By now, the office staff consisted of two assistant principals, two secretaries and one bookkeeper. We still had grades 10 to12 so he was pretty busy. I never could remember how many faculty members that we had but every time that we met, there was a sea of people, mostly women. There was a big vocational department with Construction, Bricklaying, Cosmetology, Welding,

Agriculture, Drafting and Food Service. There was a big Business department with Typing 1 and 2 (these were the days before computers), Shorthand 1 and 2, Accounting, Bookkeeping, and Record Keeping (I never did know what that course consisted of). Keeping that entire faculty happy was more than 10 men could handle. Could you imagine having 50 women just like your wife that you saw every day? The teachers were always bickering with each other and whining about this and that. A third of them were always sick with something, a third of them wanted to see him every day about this and that, and the other third had to leave early for some personal reason. It was a zoo most of the time. I tried not to get mixed up in the politics of the school and kept pretty much to myself. The teacher's lounge was a no-no for me. It was useless but you wanted to get involved in one side or the other. First-lunch teachers were always complaining about second-lunch teachers and vice-versa. I couldn't eat in the lunchroom because the food was full of starch and I loved it and boy did it put the pounds on. I tried to be selective about the meals that I ate down there. Edna never came out of her office, as I told you before, so it was a pretty lonely existence. Have I told you about William? If I have, just skip this part because I am going to tell you again.

William replaced Elma when she left. Remember, I told you about Elma, she was the one that rode the broom. She was the one that gave such a hard time. William was the 10th- grade counselor. He was huge and Black with a chip on his shoulder as big as all outdoors. We co-existed as best we could if you consider everything that was stacked against us and sometimes we were even on the same side. I wouldn't say that we were the best of friends. I guess the best way to describe him would be to tell you that when he was in the Second World War and when the troop trains rode through the south, he said all of the blacks had to pull the shades down so that the southerners would not see them. I was never sure whether or not that was because they did not want the populace to know how many blacks we had fighting for their country or whether they were afraid the black faces would incite a riot. Either way seemed pretty stupid to me but I guess that you had to have been there. There was always the outside possibility that he was lying. Anyway, he was one of those counselors who let the boys smoke in his office. If the administration caught you smoking in the building, they would suspend you. He felt that it made them feel like buddies but I hated it because to me it seemed like a flagrant misuse of authority. I started this whole paragraph off just to let you know that I didn't eat with him either.

Most of the time, I had students in my office during lunch. Sometimes we were just shooting the bull but sometimes we had really good unorganized group sessions. Sometimes I used that time to talk with teachers, who had the same lunch that I did, about their students who were having problems. Sometimes I hid out in the record room to type transcripts. Never did I enter into the lounge gossip.

Then there was Sue! Sue was hired somewhere along the way as the ninth grade counselor. She was pathetic, that's all I can say about her. She lost everything that she put her hands on, including her paycheck. She lost that almost every month. It would always turn up in the strangest places. One time, I remember they found it in the boy's bathroom. I mean, she left it there and no one stole it! It could be anywhere: the trash cans, the library, the lounge, even a classroom. She had asked the administration to issue her another check so many times that they finally made her use direct deposit. She would lose transcripts, folders, recommendations, letters, everything.

Her favorite comment was "I walk to a different drum" and believe me she did. You had to feel sorry for her and for the longest kind of time I always tried to help her out but everything has a limit. She went to Europe once with a group from school and everywhere the bus stopped she would get lost and they would have to wait and wait for her. Finally, the teachers who went to Europe with her had to take turns going with her during free time to be sure she got back on time. At one stop the bus just left her and she had to find her own way to the next town. Even that didn't cure her. She never was on anybody else's wavelength. You could talk to her and her answer was always on another subject. She would always come up with the most bizarre ideas at the meetings that we had and we wanted to quit having them just so that we wouldn't have to listen to her. You can only take so much of that kind of stuff. She ate in the lunchroom every day and that was another reason that I stayed in my office.

A teacher sent the boy to my office. She said that he had been withdrawn and hardly ever said anything in her class, even when she asked a direct question. She wanted me to see what I could find out about him. He was an honor roll student, nice looking, tall and handsome I guess you would call him. We talked for a little while but it was close to the end of the day and he rode a bus. He promised me that he would come back the next day when he could find some time. I didn't see him the next day or the next and I really forgot about the whole incident. When I saw the teacher in the hall it reminded me of him and I made myself a note to call him down on the third day.

That night I was watching the news and I saw a picture of him on the TV. He had been apprehended by the police for shooting his parents. The announcer said that he had gone home from school, taken down a shotgun that belonged to his father and shot both his mother and father. Neither one of them was dead but they were both in the hospital. I couldn't believe my ears! That sweet mild-mannered young man shooting both of them with a shotgun! I could not compute that. I would always wonder if I had called him back that next day would he still have done it. The remorse and sadness that I felt was almost unbearable. I carry that thought with me even today. I can still see his face in my mind's eye as he talked with me.

Both parents survived and the psychiatrist who evaluated him said that he was not able to stand trial and they put him in the state hospital for the insane to begin treatment. The next thing that I heard was that he was out and had gone back to live with his parents. Now I ask you, could you let someone come back to live with you if they had shot you? Even if it was my child it would have been very hard for me. You could never be sure whether or not he would do you in as you slept. I am sure that he had nowhere else to go but I felt so bad for those poor parents. He did not reenter high school and I guess that he went somewhere else to finish his education. I never heard anything else about him or his parents.

Then there was Ralph. A teacher called me on the intercom one day to come up to her room. Ralph was disturbing the class and she could not get him to leave. She didn't call the administration because she liked Ralph and she did not want him to get into trouble and she knew that something was really wrong with him. By the time that I got up there, he was raving and ranting and pacing up and down in front of the class. I knew as soon as I saw him that things had gone beyond my expertise and we were going to have to have someone to help us. I called down to the office and two of the men came up to help me get Ralph out. I finally talked him down and got him out in the hall. He seemed to calm down a little bit but as soon as the two assistant principals got there he was off again and fighting them when they put their hands on him. One of them called the police and they were at the school in five minutes. Ralph was screaming and fighting and kicking and they finally got the cuffs on him and I talked them into taking him to the mental health clinic instead of jail. I went with them to be admitted and as long as I was talking with him and explained things to him he was not too wild. We called his parents and his father promised to come down as soon as he could and we put Ralph behind lock and key until he could get there. I felt like it was drugs but I wasn't sure. Both of the policemen who came were very nice and they did not traumatize him any more than they could help. Both of them felt that he had gotten hold of some bad stuff too.

About a month after that we were playing bridge at my house one night and Ralph walked in. I did not know that he knew where I lived and it disturbed me a little bit. I could tell by his eyes that he was wild. He had not been back to school since his episode with the police and I had visited him a couple of times at the mental health clinic. He seemed to be getting along much better and they were planning to release him in about two weeks. He was talking all of this 'off the wall' wild stuff and suddenly he pulled a gun out of his coat pocket. Well, the other three girls in the living room started screaming and carrying on and I thought that we would all be shot if they didn't shut up and let Ralph settle down. I have heard of people talking in tongues at religious meetings and it sounded to me like that was what Ralph was doing then. It was about then that we heard a police siren above all of the hubbub. Ralph heard it too. He stopped brandishing the gun around, said goodbye, and ran out of the room. I don't think that my friends will ever get over the episode. Neither will I.

About a week ago Ralph walked by my house with two little children. He stopped and we talked for a long time. He said he had moved about a block from me. He said that he had married and was working for a local oil company. He said that things were going well for him. Neither of us mentioned the long-ago episode and I was glad to see that he had fared as well as he had. He looked as though life had been good to him. He had marched over That Hill.

One of the best resources that a counselor has is their eyes. Their ears and their listening ability is number one on the priority list but some of them don't use their eyes. I could always tell when a student was in need of special help just by looking at them. Their hair seems to stick out in little individual pieces going in all different directions, especially noticeable in boys. Don't laugh, this observation has never failed me. Their eyes are a dead giveaway but that hair denotes something very serious.

John had the lead role in one of the school plays and when I went backstage to congratulate him on his wonderful performance I noticed his hair. I knew that something was really wrong. I made a mental note to see him the first thing the next morning. Back in those days, I never forgot anything but that's not true now.

I finally called him down sometime after lunch. It was a warm day and he still had on his overcoat. That hair was just like it was the night before. The style then was semi-short and all of those little pieces were sticking out everywhere. We talked for a little while and his responses to my questions seemed a little disjointed and off base. His eyes wandered and he would not look at me. This was not like him. He lived about four miles from me and I had seen him all of his life. I had watched him grow into a handsome, intelligent and responsible young man. His mother taught in a near-by school and I knew her fairly well.

I watched him as he rambled. His eyes darted from side to side. I knew that he had just come back from New Orleans. A local minister had chaperoned a group of young boys, as he did every year, and they had stayed for a long weekend. I thought that I would try to get him back to reality so I asked, "Did you have a good time in New Orleans?" It was as though I had slapped him across the face.

His head snapped around and he said, "Look what he did to me, I don't want to live!"

I had always taken suicide threats seriously. I never dismissed such words or actions as attention-getting and manipulative. The first question that I always asked was, "Have you thought out a method for dying?"

"Yes, I know how I am going to kill myself", he said. "I will never be able to face anyone again after what I did in New Orleans. Death is the only way out. I was blind-sided and I did not know what he was asking me to do until it was too late. I looked up to him so. He was my mentor and I had spent time alone with him before. Oh, I want to die". I knew that his problem was beyond my ability to help him and I knew that we had to get him help that day. Hospitalization with constant supervision was the only answer.

I stepped to the door and told a student to get someone in the office to call his mother When she finally arrived, I told her that he was too depressed for me to help and that I felt that he needed medication to get him through his problems. She did not believe a word that I said and told him to go back to class and she would talk to him later.

He tried to kill himself that night by taking a whole bottle of his mother's sleeping pills. It was not the plan that he had told me about but it was close. She took him to the hospital and they pumped his stomach and sent him by ambulance to a local Private Psychiatric Hospital. He stayed there six weeks.

He is a medical doctor now, and I hear that he is a good one. I see him every now and then when he comes home. He was one of the ones that made it.

I have guessed what happened to him but I do not know for sure. I had heard tales about that minister for years. Even though the rumors were rampant, parents still entrusted their young men to his care for trips each year to New Orleans and also to religious camps. I always thought it was a dead giveaway when he didn't want to take the girls. Ministers can do no wrong and are considered perfect to people in the South. The parishioners sit them up on pedestals and almost worship them. This particular minister had been at the Presbyterian church for 32 years. He is dead now, cancer they said, but I wonder. I also wonder how many other young men had gone through the same thing that John had.

All of this is so relevant to the news of today. The papers are filled with the priest who has abused children. If there had been any Catholics in our town during those years, I am sure that I would have had some of those young people in my office but you can bet your bottom dollar that I would have reported them. It probably would have done no good but I would have been in there pitching. My counseling books would have said that these priests had missed some stage of development in their past that caused this. I guess the 'sexual development stage'. What do you think?

CHAPTER 14

The Disadvantaged and the Empowered

I was seldom ever sick. I probably didn't miss five days the whole thirty years that I was working in the school system, but I was really sick one time when I contracted viral pneumonia. I was always a little skeptical of the diagnosis because another teacher had the same thing that I did at approximately the same time and one of the teachers died about the same time of some respiratory ailment. I always thought that it was Legionnaires Disease but anyway I was in the hospital about ten days and they finally had to call some 'high faluting' doctor down from Duke to take care of me. I smoked back in those days and I caught anything that had to do with the lungs. Anyway, the reason that I am boring you with my illness is to tell you what one of my students who had a learning disability said when I returned.

He met me in the hall the first day that I was back. We had spent quite a bit of time together with one thing and another, going over his Competency work, writing out his educational plan, talking about after he graduated and stuff like that. He looked me straight in the eye and said, "I know why you got sick."

It took me so by surprise that I kind of floundered about for words. I was almost afraid to ask him why because there was no telling what he might say and there were two or three students standing with us. Anyway, I waded in and said, "Why?"

"Because you wear your skirts too short, and the bugs got in through your knees. Now you need to add some more material to your skirts so that they can't get in again."

I had done a lot of counseling with EMH students in our school. They are students who cannot be taught effectively by regular educational methods. They cannot retain what is taught them and their attention span is very, very short. They are the sweetest children in the world and it is very rewarding to talk with them. Most of them are very unrealistic, their IQ is below 71, and in those days they were not usually 'mainstreamed'. Don't let me get by with a word like that and not tell you what it means.

We could not put them in regular classes or in the main flow of things. They were in self contained classes with one teacher all day. I am sure that you think that what he said was a joke; it wasn't. I have never seen anyone as serious as he was and I am sure that he believes that to this day. I see him all of the time working in the local nursing home and he has become a productive functional member of the community. I told you earlier in this book my feelings about teaching handicapped students. His teachers made him feel accepted and a part of society in spite of his limitations and he has made a place for himself. There is a lot more to learning than books, as all of you know.

Speaking of handicapped students, have you ever witnessed controlled anger? By controlled anger, I mean someone so angry that they would throw a pocketbook across my office but there was no emotion involved in the action. You did not get the feeling that they were angry at all. I guess that you call it anger with no emotion. I did not believe that it was possible but it made such an impression on me that twenty years later I can still see her doing it in my mind's eye. I still see that mother as she hurled that pocketbook. The fact that she threw it shocked me because I had no idea that she was angry. Her facial expression had never changed.

Her son had been enrolled in our school for about a week. He was wheelchair-bound and had no use of his legs and arms. I have forgotten the name of the disease that he had, but she felt that no one was taking care of him. They would wheel him up to class and the student would leave him there when they went to their next class, forgetting him. Someone had assigned a student to take care of him each period but it was not working out. She was livid, or so she said, with a face that showed no expression. Looking back on it, she had been with this child for seventeen years like this and perhaps she had just given out of emotions except for those that were superficial. When her actions became violent, I knew that I had to do something fast. Armed with the pocketbook scene, "the powers that be" procured a sitter for the student. Sadly enough, he died about a month later and I never saw the mother again. I often wondered, if after resting awhile, had she gotten her emotions back or if she was doomed to go through the rest of her life without any. How sad!

I guess I need to take a stand here about IQ since I have talked about quite a few students with limitations. I know that research suggests that IQ is not fixed. It is not an unchanging human characteristic. Ahough the IQ does appear to become more stable over time, it can vary, and especially change during the early years. Most of the research indicates that the pliability of intelligence is greatest when a child is young and that intellectual functions develop most rapidly during the early years. Environmental influences, therefore, would have their greatest impact, either positively or negatively, during that time. I hate getting into footnotes and all of that junk but I think it was Bloom (1964), and many other researchers agreed with him, who was almost positive that by age eight, very little effect could be seen through environmental influences, either positively or negatively, on a child's IQ. If the research is right it would seem that by the time this handicapped child reaches high school, the teacher should be primarily concerned with social adjustment and self-esteem. These children are hungry to talk with an accepting individual, one who listens to them without passing judgment or laughing at them. Some of my most rewarding moments in counseling were spent with these special young people.

Educators are still arguing about whether we should have heterogeneity in our classrooms which means all different kinds of students, slow learners, fast learners, and middle of the road learners in the same class. Educators have often claimed that such heterogeneous classes represent high expectations for struggling learners, but we leave them to their own devices to figure out how to 'catch up' with the expectations. Such an approach does not result in genuine growth for struggling learners. Neither do advanced learners proceed with genuine growth. They must serve as peer coaches, or wait, patiently of course, while students with less advanced skills continue to work for mastery of skills already mastered by the advanced learner. The advanced learner does not move ahead as they should. Let's face it, Basically we are still doing things like we did 100 years ago. We adopt a single textbook and give students a single test at the end of the chapter and another test at the end of certain marking periods. We have the same grading system for all students. It doesn't matter where they started at the beginning of the year. I guess you could say that we strive to prepare students for tests more than for life.

I keep reading into the facets of education that are discussed everywhere and I wanted to keep away from all of that. However, I guess there is one more that needs to be covered here because you are going to meet some of them later. That is the students that are labeled ADHD. Those initials stand for 'attention deficit hyperactivity disorder'. When I first started counseling, I had never heard of ADHD students and it wasn't until the middle of the 1900's that they started appearing in the high school. Where did they come from? What was causing this rash of students with the same symptoms? The traits were restlessness, inattentiveness, and impulsive behavior. All school-age children and especially boys have these symptoms. Teachers were told that if these symptoms persisted for many months and seemed excessive in comparison to most children, then concern for the welfare of these children should be paramount to the teacher. If the teachers of these children were simply told to ride out the behavioral storm it would be harmful to the future academic and social adjustment of the child. Well, that's a mouthful isn't it? However, you know what they did. Medication was the answer. Had I been their teacher I would have wanted them on medication too.

I was finally convinced that it was a neurological condition. All of the mental health professionals that I have talked to have convinced me that it is neurological, something about the axons and dendrites firing differently. Remember I told you at the beginning of this book that I was trained as a biochemist. I guess in nonprofessional terms you could say that the area of the brain that regulates impulses, attention, and behavior is thought to be under-active, compared to children without the disorder. There are probably many causes of ADHD, heredity is thought to be the most common. ADHD does run in families. I think that it has been pretty well established that parenting styles or teaching strategies do not play a part in causing ADHD (Barkley, 1990). Most authors say that classrooms and social situations can affect the severity of the problem but they are not the cause.

Anyway, the reason that I started all of this is that these students started arriving at the high school in droves. I mean these students who had been diagnosed as ADHD and had been on medication since early elementary school. I started seeing them in the guidance office and it took me about a year to realize what was going on. That seems like a long time doesn't it but you know you have to ask the right questions to get answers and you have to have some insight into what's going on before you can ask them. I didn't have children that age and most of my time was spent at the school so I was clueless.

When these types of students hit high school and were struggling for independence, like most teenagers, they stop taking their medication because they did not want to be different and they felt that the medication made them different. The result was that they began having a very difficult time in the classroom and with their peers.

There was a very intelligent boy named Harold who started taking the SAT when he was a junior. I think his score came back around 650 which was very surprising in light of the courses that he was taking and the educational training of his parents. Since I was the test coordinator for the county, his parents came in to see me one day about individual testing. They explained to me about his diagnosis of ADHD and asked me to look into some special testing for him. This was before the days that the testing service allowed special testing or even knew about the existence of these students I guess. After lots of phone calls and many talks with different people in New Jersey and validated proof that Harold was handicapped, we set up some individual testing for him and the College Board allowed me to test him one- on-one. When I called Harold down and talked to him about it, he flat refused to have anything to do with it. He said that he did not want to be singled out and he only wanted to take it the way it was given to the rest of this peers.

He signed up to take the regular SAT with his classmates the following test date and since I was present at that testing, I watched him taking the test without him knowing it. It was amazing. He looked out of the window half of the time, he pulled the table back and forth, and he opened his test book and closed it at least twenty five times. He would drop his pencils, get out of his chair and pick them up. Finally, I had to reprimand him and I told him that I was going to have to remove him from the test site if he did not calm down. He put his head on his desk and marked his answer sheets without reading the questions. This was not all that unusual because a lot of students did that. When we received his test results back he made 630.

After the results came back, I called Harold down again. "I watched you taking the SAT during the last test date and frankly I was very confused", I said. "You seemed so disinterested and unfocused. Are you not planning to go to college?" Well, it was like I had slapped him in the face. "Not go to college. "Of course I am going to college. What does the SAT have to do with that," he practically screamed at me. "Don't you know that I have been labeled ADHD and I can get into college as a handicapped student just on the basis of that condition. I don't care what my parents tell you, I refuse to take my medication and I have never told them about it. Now don't you be a busybody and tell them everything that you know. I am supposed to take one pill before I come to school and one at lunch. I stopped taking them last September when school started. It is April now and I am doing fine." I called each of his teachers to find out what 'fine' was and he was failing four out of five subjects. What a waste!

We had four or five informational sessions after that. You know that kind that you dispense information on a subject and the student assimilates the information, if you are lucky. I think a long time ago they called it lecturing. I told him that he would never get into a state supported school in North Carolina regardless of his handicap unless he had 800 on his SAT. I hated to talk to him like that, but we needed to take some drastic measures.. I told him that he could hang it up for all of those schools. He told me that he had been taking medication since he was in the fourth grade and he was not going to take it again.

I finally talked him into taking the SAT with just him and me in the room. I set up the test date, received his testing materials and the instructions included no time limit on the test. I closed all of the blinds put him in the middle of the room with no desks around him, stopped the clock on the wall, and give him one pencil. I made him stop working every ten minutes and walk around the desk, stretch, and trim his pencil. It took us three eight hour days to finish the test. He scored 1100. He was so proud of himself. He agreed for his parents to come in and have a conference with us and he told them about the medication. Even if he had not done well on the SAT, I would have had to tell his parents, he knew that. In the end, after we had talked with all of his teachers about his problem, he ended up passing all of his subjects for the year. He did well his senior year and went on to become a very productive college student and is now a lawyer. I see him every now and then and he hugs me.

I guess the point that I am trying to make here is that not only do each of these students become a different person with drugs but they also develop an attitude that affects their everyday life. Every one of them that I have ever had dealings with thinks that everybody else owes them something. They have the attitude that they can order everyone around and that the 'world owes them a living' so to speak. I have often wondered if the medication is the cause of the attitude. What is causing all of these kids to appear on the scene suddenly? But that is where all of this part started, by that same question.

"Mind your own business," the mother said to me as she sat at my round table discussing her son's trouble in school. I'll take care of him at home."

His English teacher sat with us and boy, had she been caustic. She had asked me to call the conference with the mother because she could not put up with him any longer in class and she wanted him taken out and put in a slower class where he could keep up. She said she could not concentrate on teaching the other students because she spent so much time disciplining him. "He never pays attention in class, he is always making faces at the other students and he never does his homework. He has failed every test that he has taken this year and when he takes one he finishes before the other students do and does things to distract them so they cannot concentrate. It is quite obvious that he does not belong in my top classroom."

As I sat listening to them, it was quite obvious to me that I was the only one listening; I wondered who had ownership of this problem. Does that seem like a strange question to you? Well it's not and generally I feel that the person who comes to me is the one who has the problem. Problems are like 'hot potatoes'. Nobody wants to take hold of them but they have to be broken down into little pieces to solve them. The mother did not have the problem. She obviously did not care that the student acted out in the teacher's room. I surely didn't have the problem although I had the solution, move him. Was that the best thing for the student? After all, he was the customer. He was why we were there. Without him none of us had a job.

The mother and the teacher went round and round until they both were exhausted. The mother accused the teacher of not reading the student's folder. "If you had you would have known that he had been identified as ADHD and that handicap qualifies him for special attention and special treatment. There is an individualized education program in his folder." This is better known in educational circles as an IEP. "If you do not modify your classroom procedure to accommodate him, I will call the State Department and you will have a law suit on your hands."

Her psychological stage was certainly not one of acceptance. In one of those courses that I had taken somewhere along the line we had been taught that there were five emotional stages that were necessary for parents of children with disabilities to pass through in order to heal themselves and learn to cope. I think that it was Lubler-Ross in 1969 who first proposed them in her book *On Death and Dying*, and Duncan (1977) who adapted her 'grief theory' to disabled populations. Just to keep you up on everything, the stages are denial, anger, bargaining, depression, and acceptance or coping. We could go into a very good description of each of them here but I think that the names of each one are pretty descriptive on their own. Anyway, all of this preamble leads up to one place. That's how I met Harry.

I wish everybody could know Harry. When I think of how the teacher described him and how I saw him, it made me laugh. Harry was only a freshman when I met him. Usually I never saw freshmen. They were seniors before they got in my office and I was usually very protective of that status because other counselors got very angry about you talking to their students. However, the parent was the key here and I did not have a choice because she would not let me refer him or her for that matter. When I had told the teacher and the mother that I was going to talk to Harry before I made my decision, you would have thought that I had STUPID stenciled on my forehead. I knew that they were thinking, 'Now what has she got to do with this'? To me the student came first and it really didn't matter to me what either one of them thought when you got right down to it.

Harry was short and small for his age and I guessed by looking at him that he was immature. He had dark black hair and dark black eyes. "I haven't done anything wrong, why have you called me down here?" he asked. I never knew why, but some students still thought that when you got called to the guidance department it was a discipline problem. I don't know of any counselor who called a student down because of discipline. That was the principal's and the assistant principal's job, but they always asked what they had done wrong. Maybe it boiled down to the fact that they had done something wrong and they were afraid that we had found them out.

"I hate that damn teacher", Harry said when I told him why I had sent for him. "She has all of those pets in her room. They answer all of her questions and she lavishes them with her attention. There are about ten of them and none of the rest of us counts. It's like we are not even there. I'm a whole lot smarter than any of them but she hates me because I'm different. So I just act up, I guess you would say, and that way I get noticed. I don't care about passing her old course and the way things are going, I won't."

"How about letting me move you out into a lower English class. Maybe you can still salvage it and you won't have to come to summer school. It is English you know and if you don't pass you will still be a freshman next year," I said. It was like I had slapped him across the face with my hand.

"There is no way that I will let you move me out of there. She is going down with me. My mother will see to that," he said. I could just see the teacher mired up to her neck in quicksand with arms outstretched and a smile must have crossed my lips. He picked up on that immediately and accused me of not believing that the teacher would 'get it' too. I tried to explain my mental picture of his teacher but the thought was too frivolous for him and he rejected it.

"If you are so smart Harry, why are you failing?" I asked. "Is this a part of some big plan that I am failing to see?"

"Well, it's like this," he said. "She has no business ignoring me. I am supposed to get special attention. It's written in my folder and I have always had it before. I demand it now. I will not let her get by with this."

I said, "Harry, you are in high school now. Things are going to be different from elementary school and you have to 'fish or cut bait' as the old saying goes. You have to do the work or you don't get the credit for the course. Your days of getting special help in the classroom are over. Now I can get you help after class but your teachers don't have time to baby you and slow the class down to accommodate you. It doesn't matter what letters they call you by."

"You and I will talk about this later," he said. "It's time for the bell and I have English this period and I do not want to miss an opportunity to antagonize her in the classroom." Well so much for that conference, I thought. I guessed the next time that I talked to him, I would have to use a different approach. The one today certainly had not worked. I didn't know any more than I did before I called him down. I wondered if a conference with Harry, the teacher, and me would get us anywhere. It was worth a try but I felt that I should talk to him one more time before I took that drastic step. That one could backfire on me.

As it turned out, I didn't have to call him back. The next day there he was waiting for me when I got to school at 7:30.

"O. K. lady counselor, let's talk!" I wondered about this clever boy and all those initials that he had carried around him like a cloak since elementary school. I wondered how he could have gotten so side-tracked, so demanding, so cunning. I gave him the lead. "Are you on to me?" he asked.

'Perhaps,' I thought, but I only smiled. Nonverbal communication can be a wonderful thing sometime and it has always stood me in good stead. Some counselors are very uncomfortable with it but most young people love to see it because they are lectured to so much. The eyes are the giveaway to them. They read them like a book. They know a phony immediately. Where do they learn that stuff?

"I thought so," he said. "I can't stop, I don't know how. I have been doing it so long that it is a part of my personality now."

"Do you want to?" I asked him. "Because if you want to stop, you can. It's never too late. You have your whole life in front of you and so many wonderful things to see and do. I hate to see you waste all of that high level energy making other people unhappy and ultimately hurting yourself. Whose skirts are you hiding behind?"

It ended up that the teacher, Harry, and I spent two hours after school that day together. Before it was all over there were three of us crying crocodile tears. Each of them promising to take a new direction, each promising new classroom behavior, each promising to respect each other, each of them taking responsibility for their actions. How tenuous is the thread that holds us to behavior outside of our basic personalities.

Whenever I think back to things that I have experienced with young people, I always come back to genes, oh those powerful genes. Can we really do very much about them? I guess we all have problems dealing with that age-old issue.

As you know, not all things turn out as beautiful as we would like for them to. Life is not a bed of roses. Harry failed English. I guess that he was too far gone when we got to him. His mother brought the State down on the school and the teacher, but the teacher's relationship with Harry was wonderful and that was the only good thing that came out of the whole episode. Perhaps one small step is enough. It was not the last time that I saw Harry. He filled my office with his energy many, many times before he graduated. He learned a lot that year and coming to summer school was probably good for him. It upset me that the teacher did not pass him but what good would that have done.

All of the State's bluster did not amount to anything and the next year started out just like the year before. Perhaps what I wanted the reader to learn from this episode is that there are times that ADHD is not appropriate and young people who are labeled with it use it to their advantage. Years and years ago, we probably would have said that the youngster who exhibited this behavior was bored in the classroom because they were so smart. We would have tried to present them with more avenues to expand their knowledge, more things to keep them busy. Now we have whole departments in the school system for this. Is this good? I don't know, but then I am not a teacher.

I remember that I wrote a recommendation once for a student to attend Harvard. I was fairly new at counseling then. I wanted him to gain acceptance to Harvard very badly so in the body of the letter I made the statement that I felt sure that he was bored in school and that the curriculum that he had to take in our school was not very challenging. Actually, I was writing it for the principal because the form had to be signed by him. I did not trust him to write it. He read it and threw the paper straight up in the air and said, "I'll not sign that. You are talking about my school." It really surprised me and to this day, I don't see what was wrong with what I said. I rewrote it but I was never happy about it.

Speaking of teachers, there is not enough that I can say about the good ones. They care about young people, they are wonderful, and they are the first ones to spot students who have problems, ones who need help. They have saved many, many students from devastating results simply by a little referral. Sometimes it only takes a kind word, or a smile or words of encouragement. A counselor's office should always be open to them and for them. There are some teachers that are rotten. A pox on principals who let them teach our young people because it is the easy way out.

I don't know about now, but back in the dark ages, when I worked, the principals knew who they were. They could have documented what they did and gotten them out of the school system, but they didn't. They left them there to influence our young people and smother them with bad teaching. It was the easy way out for the principal. A teacher had a job as long as they wanted it unless they physically abused a student. That's a little far fetched, but there is a lot of truth in it. We had a teacher in our school that was so bad that it was a joke. He sat up in his class every day and read a novel. Now he was teaching low classes, but I ask you, who better then slow students need a good teacher. He was teaching math. He would give them a sheet and tell them to work the problems on the sheet. He gave them a new one every week and that was the extent of his teaching. Believe me he read a ton of books every year, all romance novels. He worked in that school system for ten years, ten years! It did not matter what I said to the principal or what other people said to the principal. There he sat. He got so fat that he waddled when he walked and the only way that he finally left the school system was that his back started bothering him and he got some doctor to write him up for disability. Boy did that doctor do the school a favor.

For the parent who might read this, don't let that happen. You have the strongest voice of all and you should make yourself heard. Just be sure of your facts and forge ahead. You can move mountains. I have never seen a school system that did not bow to parents' demands. The main problem is that when those teachers teach slow students, their parents are not as active in the affairs of the school and are not as comfortable making waves. Am I saying that slow students have slow parents? No, but economic and social deprivation are paramount in most of these students' lives.

CHAPTER 15

All Kinds of Problems

I have been trying for the last twenty or thirty pages to decide how to introduce you to my first really big case of mixed racial romances and I guess that the only way to do it is just to dive right in. It is complicated and explaining it to you will be very difficult. I was working late one day, my children will tell you that it was the rule rather than the exception, when a very well dressed black couple knocked on my door. It was open and I looked up thinking that I had met them before but I could not remember where. They began telling me about their son, who was a star football player, and who was very serious about a white girl. I always felt that the principal had pawned them off on me because he could not handle it, but it didn't matter because I was glad that I had met them. They talked for over an hour about the relationship and how they felt that the school should do something about it and how it was ruining their son's career. They had big plans for him and they felt that the relationship would interfere. Remember, this was a long time ago. They also felt that the people in their community were looking down on them because he had gotten mixed up with a white girl and they were not going to stand for it. She called him all of the time and came to the house every day after school when the parents were not there. His father was the assistant postmaster and the mother was a teacher. This was not a school problem but they thought it was. They wanted me to talk with the boy and the girl and the girl's parents, whom I knew, and get this thing straightened out. They wanted her to leave him alone.

Somehow I felt threatened by the situation but looking back on it, I am not sure why. Perhaps their demeanor and their demands were part of it. I knew that the school could not do anything about it. Their private lives were none of our business as long as they did not bring it to school with them. I had known about the relationship. The student grapevine told me. I promise you that student grapevine was always right and I listened to it. Anything that you wanted to know, all you had to do was ask. A lot of times, I didn't ask because I didn't want to know. It was kind of like a parent who is better off not knowing. Anyway, I listened and I listened, and I listened some more. It went on and on. The gist of the whole thing was that they did not want him messed up with a white girl. It was just that simple. She was not good enough for him. It would only cause him trouble. I told them that I would talk to both of the students and show them some alternatives, but beyond that, I could do nothing.

I did that. I tried to explain to the girl that his parents were ticked off. Why didn't they make plans to go somewhere else where the neighbors would not see them to keep piece in the family? I appealed to him to be more discreet. I tried to explain to them what they were bringing down on themselves. It was obvious to me that she ruled the roost and he was just a tag-along. She was a fiery bottle blond, and she had the attitude, 'no one will deter me from my goal'. I was not sure what her goal was but she wasn't interested in anything that I had to say. Remember, I told you earlier in this book that the 'word on the street' was 'if you had not tried it, don't knock it' well she had tried it often and she was not giving it up.

It wasn't long before the mother of the girl came to see me. She had divorced the student's father and was living with her boyfriend. Her attitude about the whole affair was not nearly as hostile as the boy's parents but she would have liked to see it all go away. Well it didn't. The boy's parents made a steady path to my office about twice a week and became more hostile with every visit. We would talk about two hours every time that they came or "they" would talk about two hours. They meant for me to do something and on numerous occasions, they made it quite clear that if I did not, they would! Finally, the last time that I saw them they stormed out of my office and said that they would never speak to me again. Perhaps I had listened too much.

Well, the upshot of the story was that he was not recruited by any professional or college team like his parents thought he would be. They did not get married. She got pregnant and had a baby girl. Her mother lives on the same street that I travel going home every day and I see her with the girl. She stays with her a lot. I do not know what either one of the students are doing now, but I know that they are not married. I think that the girl started college, she was very smart, but I do not know whether she finished or not. Life can be very cruel

I met the little girl at a funeral that I went to about a week ago. She was around thirteen years old and beautiful. Her mother was with her and she introduced me as her high school guidance counselor. She told the child that I had helped her so very much when she was back in high school. I could not think of one positive thing that I had done for her other than listening but I guess that it was all in the eyes of the beholder.

One of the strangest things that I ever had happen evolved SAT scores. It's something that every counselor, every parent, and every teacher should know about. The Scholastic Aptitude Test is a test that every student who plans to attend college has to take. It is very traumatic for students because so much hinges on high scores. Their whole lives can be affected by one little test. Well, our school was the designated test center for the whole county and I was the test administrator for thirty years. It was given four times a year at our school, usually without incident. I always followed all of the procedures dictated by the testing service and was very diligent in my duties. I always tried to make students comfortable and tried to relieve them of their test-taking anxieties. The Test Administrator did not actually give the test to the students but rather they took care of all the technicalities of the test and all of the setting up of the rooms and counting out the books and hiring the people who actually gave the test. Anything that happened out of the ordinary was the Test Administrator's problem. I do not know the procedures now, but in those days, it was usually a counselor who took on those duties.

Well, on this one test date a student came to sign in with the 'admit slip' from the testing service. The students had to send off their materials to register about six weeks before the actual test date and had to present an admit slip to be admitted to the test. If a student was not on the roster that we received from the testing service before the test date they were not admitted. It was very rare that a mistake was made by the testing service on that roster. The student's name was not on the roster. The teacher who was checking the admit slips of the test-takers called me over to look at her admit slip. The date was smudged a little and the girl said that her baby sister had spilled something on it. It all sounded a little fishy to me but I gave her the benefit of the doubt and told her that we would call the testing service to confirm her ticket. I could not read the date either. They were the final word on everything and indicated their 'buck stops here' authority with administrators and with the students. I explained to the student that we would have to abide by whatever they said and she seemed to understand. My office was down the hall from the actual test admission site but the rooms that we used to test the students were all over the school. We usually tested about three hundred students each test date. I kept the test books in the vault until I gave them to the people who would actually administer the test on the morning of the test. The vault was in my office where we kept the cumulative folders for all of the students in the school. The only door that was unlocked in the school was the door where the students were checked in for the test. That was in the lunchroom where at least 70 students were tested. I have set the stage but you are going to be surprised at what happened. I was more than surprised. I was mystified.

I called the testing service; she was not registered for that test date. Actually, she had been registered for an earlier test date but had missed the test. Aren't computers wonderful? They know everything. I explained to her that I could not admit her but she could be rescheduled for a later date. She happened to be a senior at my school and I knew her. I told her that if she would come down Monday, I would help her make the arrangements. She seemed to understand although she was a little 'puffed up'. Probably, I thought, because she had not pulled it off. I walked her to the front door of the school and she left, or so I thought. The test had started and I went off to check on my test sites. It took about fifteen minutes to check on all of the ones downstairs and about fifteen minutes to check on the ones upstairs. I was in and out of my office for about thirty minutes, getting everyone settled before I went back to balance the registration sheet with the test takers and get everything in order.

Everything was uneventful on that day. Everything tallied up. The test books returned matched all of the test takers and for the millionth time, I breathed a sigh of relief. In thirty years, I never had a problem with a book. There were horror stories about that but we were a rural and small town test site and most of our students were unsophisticated. We knew most of them anyway and I always tried to use counselors from the other five high schools on the check-in table so that we had no identification problems. The pictures on those drivers license never matched what a student looked like anyway. In the case of twins, you didn't have a prayer and stories abounded about twins switching names and the smarter one taking the test for the other twin. Anytime that I saw twins taking the test on my roster, I would be sure that that counselor from that school was there to check them in. This test date was December.

About six weeks after that test day, I received a letter from an admissions counselor at a large state supported-school in our state. It was the practice of most counselors during those days to mail out the transcripts for students from their office. This was on their letterhead envelope along with the recommendation for the student. I hope that this practice still prevails. I know that parents can put a lot of pressure on counselors about that transcript and how it belongs to the student and all of that but stick to your guns. The student will get one when he graduates.

This admissions counselor was asking me about one of my students who had mailed her own transcript to the school along with her SAT score. The counselor got in touch with me only because she knew me and knew that I would not give that to a student. Now that SAT score comes to the high school with a sticker that the counselor sticks on the students test card in the cumulative folder. A copy of that test card usually goes with the transcript, especially if it will help the student gain admission.

When the student takes the SAT, they code in the schools that they want the Testing Service to send their SAT scores. Sometimes if the student did not do that, schools would accept those scores from the counselor. I understand that does not happen now and I am glad. Anyway, the second page of the letter showed a transcript for.... you guessed it, the girl that I would not let in the SAT that day. The transcript was beautiful. The name was the girl's. The grades were not hers. A SAT sticker was on a test card that was included with the transcript. Her name was on the sticker but the scores were not hers. I don't think that I have ever been more surprised in my life.

The girl had transferred from our school to another school outside of the county after Christmas and I had not seen her since the SAT incident. I spent almost a month trying to track down a student in my files whose SAT scores matched the transcript in that letter and I finally found it. Somehow, that girl had taken the original name from the transcript and the SAT score and mailed it with her application. It was a professional job and I don't think that you could have noticed it even with a microscope. The only thing that I ever pieced together was that the student had come back into the school. Perhaps she did not close the front door completely when I walked to the door with her, leaving it cracked. She had returned and gone into the guidance department, gone through the secretary's desk, and that student's folder had been in the desk where the secretary had typed a transcript for her and had forgotten to return it to the vault. Maybe the secretary had not finished with it. The girl had copied the transcript and test card on the copy machine in the guidance office. This was all done in the 15 minutes that I was gone checking the test sites. What would she have done if I had come back in and found her? What would I have done? I think about that episode often and somehow I feel that I was responsible. You can never be careful enough to cover all eventualities.

It reminded me of having your pocketbook stolen. It happens in the flash of an eye. One minute it's there and the next minute it's gone. It is gone so fast that somehow you can't believe that someone took it. At first, you think that you left it somewhere and then you're not sure and for days you still have the feeling that you left it lying around and it's your fault. It's crazy! I once heard a tale of a guidance counselor accidentally throwing a SAT book in the trashcan behind the school. You have to tally up after you give it. Books given out equals books taken up equals books not used. It all totals up to books received and all that stuff. They threaten you within an inch of your life. They don't want a book to get into the hands of a test taker. Anyway, I don't believe for a minute that the counselor threw that book in the trashcan. Somehow, she miscounted the books when they were taken up and some student made it out of the test center with a book. I'd bet a year's salary on that.

Dick was one of those true success stories. The kind that dreams are made of. The kind that keeps replaying over and over in the paper, on the streets, in the community and everywhere that I go. How wonderful to be faced with the results on such a continuous basis.

I first saw him in the fall of his senior year. He came into my office with one of his friends that I had known for quiet a while. He was a football player. There was something about him, perhaps shyness or lack of self-confidence, which reminded me of a teddy bear. (As they said, I could mother them to death). His friend said, "Mrs. Jones, Dick wants to go to college, can you help him?" Dick never said anything. He just nodded his head. I saw it in his eyes. The desire was there. I love eyes, don't you?

We spent hours looking for a school that would take him. I talked to the football coach to see if he could walk on somewhere and make the team. This would mean that he would be able to eat at the training table and this would save him a bundle of money. I told him to have his parents come up to see me and we would talk about financial aid. He had told me that his father was a spiritual minister. I never was quite sure what that meant but I did know that he had never been to school or had any training to be a minister. He just had a calling. It turned out that they were the sweetest people that I have ever met. There was no car but they caught a taxi to the school and met with me. I was never so embarrassed in my life. Had I known that there was no car, I would have gone to their trailer. Neither one of them had finished high school. They were so excited about Dick going to college. College for him had never entered their mind.

I knew, as soon as we finished filling out all of the financial aid papers, that he would get full financial aid. Now what that means is three fourths of the bill would be paid by the federal government and the rest would be given in work-study and loans. After four years of this, the loans could amount to a wad of money. The student owes the money because they sign the promisary note. I went through all of this with them and told them that we would cover all of the bases to find all of the scholarships that we could for him.

He was accepted at a pretty good state supported school and many local scholarships came in for him. He made the football team as a walk on and did not need the loan that he was given. I know that he did not have any spending money but he did have some friends who went there and he got to come home with them once football was over.

Every year for the next four years, his parents came back, we filled out his financial aid papers and every year he got just enough to stay in school. You have to keep a C average to continue to receive financial aid and he squeezed by that. He played football for four years and he graduated. He sent me an invitation to his graduation and I went. I was as proud of him as his parents were.

It was not too long after he graduated that he became the head football coach at a high school in our county. He has been in that position for as long as I can remember. He has won I don't know how many state championships and he is one of the most respected coaches in the state. Every time that I see him, he always tells me that he owes it all to me, Boy do I eat that up. Wouldn't you?

CHAPTER 16

Cheerleaders

Then there was cheerleading! I know that every girl who has ever been a cheerleader is going to take exception to this little piece but I must talk about it. Everyone, whether parent, counselor, principal, teacher, everybody in the world should know about cheerleaders. You could take all of the racial riots, fights, and confrontations and add them all together and it would not surpass one squabble that the cheerleading squad could have, for example, over the length of their skirts. When you take girls who say, "The only thing that I want to do with my life is be a cheerleader" and put them all together to get along, it spells trouble with a capital 'T'. Also, and I don't know why, but cheerleaders' moms are the worst meddlers in the school system.

These girls are always precious and they know it. They have beautiful legs and beautiful bodies and they use all of the above to win anything that they set their minds to. They are conniving, manipulative, saccharin sweet, and they will get their way or break down into a puddle of tears that would sway any man's heart to their way of thinking in an instant. Deliver me! If that doesn't work, they will call in the big guns, their moms. Now those women will ride roughshod over anything or anybody that stands in their precious angel's way. Precious angels, my foot!

All of the cheerleading squads that I ever had any dealings with knew that their counselor, me, did not stand shoulder to shoulder with them on most of their little deals that they tried to pull. Now that's a little reversal role, isn't it. I have always been a firm believer in the fact that you have to be responsible for your actions. If you are going to do something that is not on the up and up and you are hell bent, then you must be willing to take the consequences of your actions if you are caught. That makes sense, doesn't it? As individuals, these girls were great, but put them all together, well I have said that before. Let us take one little episode that I remember out of the hundreds that I became involved in.

I think that maybe it all starts with the tryouts. I started out as one of the judges in my early years just to help the poor coach that the principal picked to head up these angels. Little did that coach know that she would be reduced to a blot of grease before the end of her tenure. Well, at first, the girls who were on the team did not have to try out. The slots of the graduating seniors were filled with eighth graders who were coming up into the ninth grade. Now bear in mind that all of these goings-on are probably over thirteen girls out of a school of 1500 students. Anyway, the girls who were on the team were also on the judging committee. You usually had a list of attributes that you marked the girls on who were trying out on a scale of one to ten, ten being the highest. You then tallied up the votes for each girl and the girl who got the most votes was selected to the cheerleading squad. Simple isn't it? You can bet your zippy there was nothing simple about that selection.

I need to tell you also that we had added the ninth grade by this time. Every cheerleader had a special friend she wanted on the squad, or they all had a friend they wanted. The whole thing was made up of cliques and during the summer, they were all busy thinking up ways of getting that special friend on. It didn't matter if she weighed 200 pounds and could only jump one inch off the ground. That is an exaggeration because they only had thin friends who had been taking gymnastics with each other for at least four years. In addition, most of them had long blond hair. Now don't lose sight of the fact that four eighth grade schools were feeding into the high school. Some of them were riding buses to school and it took them an hour just to ride one way. These students had no idea what was going on. They didn't know diddly, much less any of the girls on the team. Well, I can tell you right now that those girls could have stayed home and watched TV because they did not have a prayer of getting selected.

There I sat, conscientiously marking my sheet and watching those beautiful girls doing their stuff. It was always very obvious, to me at least, who was good and who looked horrible. Those who had that special talent were always very easy to pick out. The first year I did not understand why not everyone saw things as I did, but I did not spend too much time dwelling on it. I was too busy. The next year I got a little suspicious and by the third year, I knew that something 'smelled in Denmark', I wonder where that saying came from? My friend says it's from Hamlet. Those first two years there was not a black on the team. Our school was 35% black. All of the cheerleaders were from the same town and the most damaging thing was that they were all best friends. They had attended the same elementary school, the same middle school, and they all took gymnastics from the same teacher. I should have left well enough alone but I was really getting ticked off about all of the good girls who never had a chance. I asked to see the voting sheets that third year. I asked the coach to bring them to the principal's office and we would go over them together. That particular year there were ten returning cheerleaders who were judges, then, there was the coach, two teachers and me. Fourteen judges were present. We were picking three girls to fill the slots of the graduating seniors. Ten of the ballots had three girls marked the same way, the highest you could get for every attribute, and the cheerleader judges had not put a mark for any other girl. The girls name was at the top of a sheet but not a number was on the ballot. There were only four ballots that had been marked conscientiously for every girl. There was no way that those three girls could have lost.

When those girls were confronted by the principal for stuffing the ballot boxes, so to speak, they dissolved into a flood of tears that would have floated a battleship. They all rushed to call their mothers to come to the school and what a mess. It ended up by that spineless principal apologizing for accusing those angels of something wrong. He did instruct the coach to bring the ballots to him each year and he would do the counting. Ha! The meeting did bring about some changes in cheerleading. Two teams were picked the next year, one for fall sports and one team for spring sports. I never judged a cheerleading tryout again. I did have some group guidance sessions later in life with cheerleading squads where we dwelt with really deep subjects like length of skirts, number of games they could miss, number of times to jump, where to stand, which color to wear or which pompom to shake.

When they were not with their group, most of these girls were sensible, caring and responsible individuals. I loved talking to them and they were just like the rest of the students.

CHAPTER 17

Gangs

I guess that this brings the conversation around to '*gangs*'. Now I know you would not equate cheerleaders with gangs but some of the same properties are there. Everyone wants to belong, and children who are attempting to belong somewhere are easy targets for gang recruitment. Sadly, they do not realize that once they get into a gang, quitting is rarely an option. Other children join gangs to gain a sense of identity. Students who feel unsafe sometimes join a gang in order to be protected.

Educators need to be alert and follow warning signs that a student may have become involved in a gang. Most of you are familiar with the warning signs; a drop in academic performance, the use of a nickname that has questionable meaning, changes in clothing, changes in friends, signs of drug or alcohol use, and a decrease in school attendance are just a few. Gang-members are usually recruited from the rising ninth grade classes when many feeder schools are feeding into a large high school. Students are afraid and want to be a part of something. They don't want to get pushed around in the hall and they don't want to eat lunch alone. That eating lunch alone is one big deal and it carries over to adulthood. Think about it. Do you like to eat lunch alone? Not me. When new students transferred into our school, one of the first things that I did was find them someone to share lunch. If they could stick together just through lunch for a while, that new student might adjust without too much trauma and make a place for themselves.

I wonder if any of you reading this know what a '*Redneck*' is. Well the kids define a redneck as a boy (there are no professed girl rednecks) who wears white socks, drives a pickup truck and has a gun rack in the back window. Sometimes he has running lights on his running board, sometimes not. He usually wears large high top boots, and his hair is cut real, real short, almost a buzz cut. Boy is he tough, or so he wants the world to think. These are also known as 'Good Ole Boys'. They represent a southern gang. A nice one, but they are a gang nonetheless. I have seen them go into action against other gangs and I definitely would prefer to be on their side most of the time. You have to look tough to be in that gang. I'll come back to this later but I want to describe to you here all of the gangs that I was familiar with in our rural and small town large school.

If you were small of statue, skinny and very sensitive you could be recruited by the 'Demon Gang'. That's what I called them. They practiced witchcraft, wore black all of the time, had pitchforks and six-pointed stars as symbols. They went around drawing these on everything. They would always sit in a circle and mumble. They usually let their hair grow real long and they were very serious about all of the witchcraft that they practiced.

Then there was the 'Baggy Pants' gang or perhaps you would call them 'sagging pants'. Sometimes you could actually see their crack above their pants. This gang started with the blacks long ago. They wore Afros then, I think that its corn rows now, and lots of jewelry. They wouldn't have had this on at Raz's school but there was no dress code at my new school and actually, I think that the administration would have said that we didn't have gangs in our school! Bull!! When a principal refuses to admit that he has gangs in his school, I think that he simply fears that such problems would be interpreted as negative reflections on his management abilities. This kind of behavior encourages gang-related activities because gang members believe that they can operate without consequences for their behavior.

This Baggy-Pants gang could be bad. They loved to bump white students in the hall and push them to one side. They would set a course in the hall and knock anyone who got in their way aside, especially if they were white. This got really bad and the whites resented the hell out of it. It probably did more to keep racial relations at a fever pitch than anything else did that ever happened at the school. It would have been so simple to stop if the principal had addressed the issue. He could have called an assembly at the beginning of the school year and explained clear rules and expectations for what behaviors would be allowed at school and what behaviors would not be allowed. Students who followed the rules would be recognized for doing so. Students who did not follow the rules would be subjected to immediate consequences. During 'passing times', problem behavior is always exceptionally high. This is the time when students have unstructured periods like going to the lunchroom and to the bus. He could have utilized additional hall monitors and had the teaching staff step to the doorways during passing times as well as before and after school. Video equipment should have been installed in the hallways and every time someone pushed another student in the hall, they would have been turned over to a mediation team of their peers to deal with the problem. If it happened a second time, another type of punishment could have occurred.

Another type of gang that we had was the 'Nazi Gang'. These boys were usually fairly good-looking, jet black hair, if not born with it they dyed it, hard nosed and regimented. They drew the swastika on all of their books and on the wall if nobody was around to see them. They hated all races but the whites and went around all of the time asking people what their religion was. There were not many of these students in our school but they made a loud noise. Sometimes it was hard to tell these gang members from the demon gang members except they drew different pictures. I am not sure those demon people hated every other race like the Nazi people though.

Then there was the 'Fellowship of Christian Athletes'. You say that is not a gang. Well it was and it was as far removed from what I perceive Christians to be as anything that you will ever see. Maybe I have the wrong idea about what Christians are. I do not think of the Crusades and the way that they killed all of those people and I do not think of the Old Testament. However, I do think of people who care about other people, who would give all that they have to a friend in need, who fill their life with love and treat others, as they would like to be treated. I do not think of them as people who necessarily go to church, but what do I know? I do know that this bunch of people who called themselves the Fellowship of Christian Athletes were clique-ish, rude and banded together to run roughshod over anybody who got in their way. They ruled the school, or so they thought, and I hated what they did to some loners. There were some really good kids in it but I hated what they did in that group. Jocks can be tough anyway. They have an image to protect and they don't like to let their guard down. I think one bad egg in a group like that who is really big and tough sets the tone for the group and the rest just won't stand up to them.

Then you have the 'Nerds'. Now that group is filled with very intelligent young people who study all the time and know it all. I don't have anything against intelligent people but they don't have to put other people down all of the time. It's like a really good bridge player who plays with someone who is just learning. They scream and cuss the beginner for making mistakes and I ask you, what good does that do? It makes the beginner feel bad and makes them never want to play bridge again. Give me the good old 'c' student; they end up running the world anyway.

Each of these gangs had little splinter gangs, kind of like churches that fell out and went off and formed their own group. It usually was because someone wanted to be the leader and could not so they got part of the members to go off with them so they could lead. Anyway, I want to talk about what happened when the 'Good Old Boys' or Rednecks met the Baggy Pants people in the hall. Now a Good Old Boy is not going to let a Baggy Pants member push him out of the way. The Baggy Pants might get away with it if the Good Old Boy is by himself and one of the smaller members of the gang, but if two or more Good Old Boys are together, the Baggy Pants leave them alone. Well, you know where I am going. That is the kind of thing that starts gang wars in schools. Just a little thing like pushing can start a major riot. Everybody thinks its big stuff, but it is not, and once the trouble starts, it is hard to get a handle on it.

Anyway, Jason, who was a Good Old Boy, truck, gun rack and all, got pushed one day in the hall when he was by himself going to lunch. Two Baggy Pants kind of hemmed him in and pushed him into a wall. They pushed him so hard that it knocked one of his teeth out. The gauntlet was thrown and the deal was that the two gangs would meet behind the gym the next afternoon after school. When a rumble like that is going down everybody hears about it and people could have made a lot of money if they had sold seats. The administration called every law enforcement officer, every fire truck, and every ambulance in the county to be there that afternoon.

Naturally, with all of the notoriety, the fight never occurred. None of them showed up. Not a single student showed their face. Somehow, Jason's name got batted around about being the instigator. He was the instigator of what? Nothing ever happened but he was called in and the administration threatened to expel him if he did not tell the names of all of the members of his gang.

All they had to do was to go look in the parking lot of the school and see who had trucks but they tried to make it something sinister. This gang was not organized like you think of gangs. There was no president or secretary. They did not have meetings or induct new members. They didn't even have an official roster. When Jason told them all of this, they did not believe him and off he went to jail. Administrators can be such assholes sometimes. I had to get a lawyer friend of mine to threaten the school system with a lawsuit if they didn't let him go. His family didn't have that kind of money and he had 'early work release' to have enough money to buy gas for the truck. The school ended up letting the whole episode drop and went right back doing the same old thing with their heads stuck in the sand.

Our high school was what I call big, you know over 1500 students. I know that many high schools have over 4,000 now but back then 1500 was considered tremendous. Why, most of the time we graduated 365 seniors. We now had grades 9-12. We were trying to move from neighborhood schools to consolidation and what a mess to put all of those warring schools under the same roof. I can remember me telling all of the parents in meeting after meeting how wonderful it was going to be. We could have all kinds of Advanced Placement courses and all kinds of special courses like journalism, leadership, welding, drafting, anatomy and psychology and stuff like that. I lied! It was not wonderful. It makes me cry to think of all that those beautiful children gave up when they left their community schools.

It is my personal feeling that once a high school size passes 400 students, it is too big. That number is ideal with grades 9-12. Surprisingly, the marginal academically struggling students come from low socio-economic backgrounds that have the most trouble. It is always the most vulnerable kids who are at the greatest risk. They seem to get lost in the shuffle in a big school. In a small school, those kids are needed. When you have a whole world of events, everybody has to participate, no matter how marginal they are. Even in sports, coaches prowl the halls looking for people with even the slightest bit of potential like having two arms. In a large school where you have to try out for everything, even chorus, the marginal people never do and you always have a whole lot more losers than winners anyway.

I think that the fact that these kids are no longer included, no longer are they a part of a group with pride in their school because they belong and are actively participating in school activities, causes drug and alcohol abuse, alienation, and delinquency. This lack of belonging and being included can be devastating to a child's psychological and social development. These kids are your 'c' students. Most of the time they end up running the world if given the chance. They have common sense, street savvy, and what I call good old 'know how'. It was one of my greatest joys to be able to counsel with them. I hope that I was a positive influence for some of them. Every child needs to be loved, valued, and shown acceptance. This is what leads to a positive identity. There is not a child living that does not want to be something or somebody. The most important thing that parents can give a child is the investment of their time to let the child know that they are accepted

I read in the paper just the other day about an integration issue that made me jump for joy. It seemed that the board of education was trying to close down an elementary school. The school was 95% black but was a neighborhood school. The parents in the neighborhood "took arms against a sea of trouble", so to speak. They marched on the board and stood them down. They did not want their children taken from their neighborhood and bused forty-five minutes down the road. Maybe there is still hope. Maybe some people are realizing the importance of the child staying near home. The verdict is not in yet. I do not know whether they can keep it open but at least they gave it their all.

I started all of this lecturing to tell you about Jim. I know that every counselor has a Jim in his or her life. Mine worked the night shift at the textile mill, Burlington if you are interested. He came to school all day, god knows when he slept, and that was the reason that the trouble started. He stayed in trouble with his teachers because he slept in class. Now I know that teachers cannot let students sleep in class and I know that they cannot make exceptions. However, for some reason, out of the six teachers that he had, the same two always sent him to the office. Bitches! I had been in the office four or five times and had seen him waiting for the assistant principal to do whatever it was that assistant principals do to students who sleep in class.

Anyway, this time I asked the assistant principal if I could take James back to my office with me and see if I could find out the problem. Boy was he glad to get rid of Jim. He said that he would have to suspend Jim because this was about the tenth time that he had been sent down and there was nothing else that he could do with him. Jim blurted out that he did not want to be in this dammed old school anyway and he just thought that he would drop out. That made me nervous. 'Drop out' was two of the words that I feared most and I would do practically anything to keep a child in school. Now I ask you, what chance does a kid have without any education? They cannot even get in the army now without a high school education or a GED.

That stupid principal said, "Don't threaten me boy, good riddance, you have caused nothing but trouble." The thing that struck me here was does "sleeping in class" classify as nothing but trouble? "We don't need you here anyway. I am calling your parents to let them know that you are suspended and when you finish in HER office hit the road." 'We' don't want you here?' I always wondered who 'WE' was, but I never found anyone who knew. I had gotten used to the 'HER' by then and the reference did not bother me anymore. He said it as if I was something dirty that he had to tolerate. However, he had used it so much that it had lost its effectiveness.

It took a lot of questions to find the bottom line with James. The blame fell so many places other than James. Of course, the teachers caught it first. It was their entire fault if they would just leave him alone. Then it was his parents because they did not make enough money. They were both on welfare and they didn't even want him in school anyway. Then it was his friends who all had cars. Then it was his girlfriend who was going to break up with him because he had no wheels. On and on it went. I have never seen a student make so many excuses for his behavior. Through all of this, he tried to make me feel sorry for him. Poor little James, having to work all night and come to school all day. Then, everyone was taking advantage of him. Round and round the mulberry bush we went and finally, after what seemed like a day, we got down to what James wanted to do with his life and how he wanted to succeed.

The upshot of the whole thing was that James kept his job at the mill. After I talked with his supervisor, who by the way did not even know that James was still in high school, he agreed to let James work the 3-11 shift. I got him released from his last class and he left school an hour earlier to get to work. It left little time for homework but then James did not need to do much in the homework line. He was a math whiz.

Most of the cases that I have come in contact with, take so little to get them back on track. However, the effort usually has to be made outside of the classroom and that means an extra effort on the part of those who help young people, beyond the regular school day. Therein lays the problem. When the bells ring, we all want to go home. Go home to our children, our family, our friends, and our life. However, you cannot, not if you want to make a difference. You also have to have a persuasive nature, a self-confidence and knowledge of the people that control the fate of young people. You have to believe that what you are proposing is right for that student and never wavier in your argument. You are not always right and sometimes you are going to make an even worse mess for them but you have to be proactive, you have to do something or lose them. You have to act, fall on your face, then get up and start over.

He kept the mill job until he graduated and with the help of financial aid, he finished college. I kind of lost touch with him but he was a success story and there are not many of those. He made it. One thing that I am sure of is that he is not on welfare.

CHAPTER 18

Letters

I saved every note that a student ever wrote to me. I have a filing cabinet full of notes. I never intended to share them with anyone, that is not why I saved them, but I would like now to share them with you here. I hope that if any student ever reads this and sees their note in print they will realize that I have shared the note with loving care and with the hope that it might help someone else. I think that the people who wrote them will understand and know that I was not breaking a confidence. Two notes are quoted verbatim because they represented a general feeling among the students in my school. The notes came from different students but one leads to the other.

> *'What I come to talk to you about is that. Well as you remember Will. Well he's starting to like me in a way where he wants me to bear his child which I'm not ready to do. And I know its' wrong but I still have a little something for him. But not in that way. I've tried not thinking of doing it and doing it. Well not doing it*

is winning and what makes it so bad is that he wants me to do it at school and to lose my virginity (our little secret, Tell no one) His girlfriend now lost her baby and he wants me to try for a baby for him instead of her.

See you,

Love"

'Dear Mrs. ...

My school year sure hasn't been what I thought it would be, When I quit school and came back it was the best thing that ever happened to me: It made me proud of myself to be able to show my family I wasn't just another high school dropout. I want to be able to have something for me and my child. First, I move out of the house with my mom because we can't get along because she puts a man before me that once tried to mess with me so me and my baby move in with my uncle and I agree to help him out but then he starts back to drinking and he comes in every night cussing at me and causing me and my child much more disturbance. I then go off with some friends to the mall and they get caught stealing and because I'm with them I get found guilty of aiding and abetting and then I have 225 hours of community service from 3 to 5 every day after school plus I'm still trying to go to school daily from 8-3 and then Johnston Tech for 150 hours of Eng. from 7-9 weekly. I left my uncle and had to move back with my mom. I hate staying here. Things haven't gotten any better there only worse. When my mom was jobless I used to ask her to keep my baby for me when she's sick day care wants you to keep them home but my mom would say she wasn't feeling well so I have to stay home and watch my own child. When my car is broke down I don't have anyway to take my baby to day care and I have to stay home and keep my own child. I hate staying so many days out of school but it's my child and I have to do what I have to do. Sure I want to graduate and make my daughter proud of me be proud of myself but I also feel like giving up Ms. Jones, like just saying forget it all and sometimes I feel like turning to drugs and alcohol and I never tried it all my life. I feel so depressed and most likely I know I want graduate this year but it seems like no one cares but you Ms. Jones your the only one that has tried to help me and I really need your help now because I do want to graduate and be able to have something for me and my child I would like someday to be a nurse so I can make money for my child and she want have it rough like me her mother (I need to talk to you because I think I'm going to quit.)

Sincerely"

Now I am sure that most of you who are reading this book probably came from a middle class background, or better, and I am sure that these notes sound foreign to you, or maybe even fabricated. When I first started counseling, I could not believe that what I heard was real. Nobody that I knew thought that way, nobody that I had ever associated with addressed problems liked these notes implied. They are real, believe me. The really difficult thing is that when you are dealing with young people, you cannot tell them what to do. You do not succeed that way. You have to educate them first and as I have told you before, try to teach them to make wise decisions. One of the best ways is to have a peer of theirs in the counseling session. Even if the peer feels the same way that they do, hearing someone else say it usually opens avenues for discussion that may lead to understanding. If the girl who wrote the first note could talk to the girl who wrote the second note, understanding would occur and she could believe the pitfalls that occur when young people have children. The boy in the first note will be gone as soon as he gets what he wants and the boy in the second note has been gone since the baby was born.

In the first note she says 'he' wants to do 'it' in school. It's true they, do 'it' in school. They have been caught in the boy's bathroom, the auditorium before school starts, the lunchroom after school, the gym behind the bleachers, and even in empty classrooms after school. Why you ask? The boys who participate in this kind of behavior do not have cars. They ride the bus to and from school. They really do not have a home to do 'it' in. That leaves school as the place of choice. There is not enough personnel in the whole school to police every area all of the time that could be used for screwing. People get real upset when they hear of something like that happening on the school grounds. They always want to know where the staff was. How could something like that happen? It is just plain dumb luck that more of them are not caught.

The girl in the second letter did finally quit school. The last that I heard from her, she had gotten on welfare and was sitting on her front stoop. I would like to tell you that she became a nurse, broke the circle, had money, and looked after raising her child but…

> *Mrs.…*
>
> *I got to talk to you. Every time that I come in somebody is with you sitting there. This is important. Please see me as soon as you are vacant. I can't make it unless you talk to me. Dalan, you remember him. He came into my bedroom last night and told me that if I didn't quit studying and making all of those good grades and Brown nosing the whites they would get me. I have never fit in. The whites don't accept me and the blacks are*

mad because I study. Help. He is serious. I have Honors Biology next period get me from there.

Mrs....

I know that you are busy but gotta see you. This school is grating on my nerve. I just might do something stupid. Try to talk me out of it. Now.

Mrs....

How do I get it through his notty head that I haint going to screw him. No way. He just wants to make me have his baby because he wants to be top dog with his friends. He makes me sick and I keep telling him to leave me the hell alone. I need help. I in English.

Mrs.

I did it again. Even after I told you I wouldn't. I feel like a heel after we talked about it. When I spit on the pizza I thought about what you said and all but I still did it. You know, what made me think that my spit was bad and all. I think that we need to talk again.

Help

Do I need to explain this one? For those of you who are living in the Dark Ages. Maybe I had better. When the Pizza boy delivers your Pizzas, if he is black and you are white and he has a chip on his shoulder, he may spit all over them before he takes them to your door. Now this action says a lot about the person who is doing this, or at least it does to me. I mean, about how he feels about himself. Anyway, that is what this note is talking about.

Mrs.

I am so unhappy, so very unhappy. I do not feel that I belong anywhere. My race does not like me. Your race does not like me. Where do I go to escape this feeling? Will I have to carry this with me forever? Why can't I belong somewhere? I do not have any friends, no one to talk to and every time I come down here you are busy so I end up writing a note. I bet that you have a desk full of notes from me. Do you keep them? I know that you told me that even writing a note helped me think through things but it just doesn't work. Call me down today. Today!

Mrs.

I'm quiten that damn job. All they do is make me work from sun up to midnight and I don't get nothing. How am I going to make the payments on my car?

See me

Mrs...

Where in the hell are you. You always gone. I'm always leaving notes and I need to talk aabout that ass hole again.

I'm in shop

Mrs. ...

This baby is gona kill me. I want to go home and they won't let me. They are so stupid. Help me.

Mrs. ...

Get your white ass upstair and get me. I'm going to kill that woman.

Mrs. ...

I'm tired of looking for you. I think I will find me somebody else to talk too. You suck.

Mr. ...

I guess you know Roy and I did it last night. It all over school that black boy went and told everyone. What should I do?

Mr. ...

I give up. You left me two days. I have looked for you. Have you left us. You sick?

CHAPTER 19

Another Principal

You know, when I whipped back through this material to see what I had left out, I could not find where I had described my principal of twenty years to you. I thought that was very interesting. I spent a quarter of my life with him and I did not tell you about him. He was a good principal. He was smart enough to let his good teachers run the school. He used all of his staff to help him hire new people. Five or six teachers and I would all meet them and talk with them and then he would ask us what we thought before he told them anything. We made mistakes but most of the time, we did a good job.

However, back to my principal. He was kind of short. He had jet black hair, squint eyes, but was nice looking. He looked a little like he had Mexican blood in him. I would have never called him progressive but he listened to his staff and moved forward, even if it was at a snail's pace. He had a nice build, dark eyes but he was not the kind of man that would ever be warm to anyone. He was good with parents because he would always listen to what they had to say and in education that is very unusual. Teachers have a way of talking down to parents. I think that it is really because they are afraid of them and they talk in all of that garbled educational gook so the parents will not understand what they are saying. Anyway, he would listen to the parents, do his homework, make a decision and get back with them. You can't ask for much more than that. It took me almost a year to get through those squint eyes.

He had an assistant principal that he brought with him from his previous school and I did not get along with him even a little bit. Looking back on it, there might have been a power play there that I was unaware of. It was the good old boys thing with the two of them. You know, back slapping, dirty jokes, tobacco chewing, the coach thing. I think that the assistant principal knew that if he gave me an inch, he would be out in the cold. He was too crude for that school. I really think that he was a little sadistic when he dealt with young people. As I have said before, without them he didn't have a job.

Each year I would write up all my goals for the next year, include all my objectives and methods for achieving them. Add all my, 'what I will do and what I will not do' and turn it in before I left for the summer. I am sure that he never read it until something would come up like a teacher who had to leave and they would call me to substitute for her until she got back. I would refuse because if you do it just one time, as a counselor they will call you every day and you will never get your work done. I would always refer them to my job description and what I would and would not do. The principal always backed me up. It took a lot of little things added up together before we were in the same pocket. You have to have your principal in your pocket if you are going to really help young people.

He knew that I worked hard, that I loved young people, and that I would back him up whenever I had the opportunity. We respected each other and we needed each other to make a good school. As I told you, he was an old coach but he finally struggled out of that role and became a principal and a damn good one! Once in a while, he still made some crazy decisions. Like the egg throwing incident but I think that the assistant principal provoked that.

Even when I was in high school in that town, the seniors always egged the juniors' cars. They usually waited until the cars were at the junior's home and did it late at night but this one time they did it on the school ground while the juniors were decorating for the junior-senior prom. I guess that they figured they could get more cars at one time and save on eggs.

That principal decided that he was going to stop that tradition or else. The next day he called down about five students at a time to grill about the incident so he could find out who was responsible. Of course, he called me down to sit in on the drilling. He told the students that whoever was responsible would not be able to attend the Junior-Senior Prom.

My daughter was in the second round of students who were called down and I found myself wishing that she had done some of the egging because I remembered that I had when I was in high school. It was always strange to me that the children of teachers or principals or counselors always seemed to walk a narrow path because they do not want to bring shame or cause any hardships for their parents. It is not something that you discuss with them but I think that they feel the burden of responsibility much stronger than the parent does. Anyway, she passed muster, the principal kept drilling, asking questions of each group of students but no one ever ratted on anybody, and I knew just as good as I was sitting in his office that every student that he called in knew who had done it. It all seemed so stupid to me to try to convict students for something as trivial as that. Attack the big things but let the little things lie. I know that half of the people reading this will not agree with that but young people have a hard enough time growing up as it is. They need a little breathing space.

The upshot of the whole thing was that he did find out. When he came to school the next day, he knew and he banished the students from the prom. Parents flocked to his office but to no avail. His mind was made up. Therefore, ten students and their dates had a prom of their own.

CHAPTER 20

And So It Goes

A friend of mine had a maid whose son went to my school. His name was Verdell. I saw him eating lunch every day with some very questionable young people. You know the kind that said it's not cool to study and make good grades and they ostracize you if you do. They were not bad boys, just not motivated. He was a freshman and I did not deal with freshmen but since I knew his mother, I thought that I would talk to him and see if I could get him started out on the right track.

We talked about the courses that he should take, his four-year plan, what he wanted to do with his life and stuff like that. He was a very good-looking boy, tall, well built but he didn't have the look of an athletic. His grades in the middle school were fair but nothing to write home about. He told me that the only thing that he had ever thought about was being on a boat and sailing across the ocean. He wanted to see things and places that he had never seen before. I am not sure but I think that I remember that he had never been out of our county. We talked about all of the ways that he could accomplish this like joining the Navy or the Coast Guard. I so wanted him to go to college but every time that I brought it up he nixed the idea. He kind of shrugged it off. We talked about the difference between an enlisted man's navy and a first lieutenant's navy but to no avail. I was only hoping that he would sign up when he registered for the courses that I had put on his four-year plan. I talked to him about twice a week for the next three weeks. Then it was registration time.

I pulled his registration sheet and he had not signed up for a single course that I had put down; no math, no foreign language, no college prep, anything. Shop, PE, weight lifting, and stuff like that were on his sheet. I am here to tell you that I sat right down and changed everything that he had on it. Sometimes it pays to do some directive counseling. I took the sheet to his mother and told her what I had done and she signed it. He moved heaven and earth to drop and add courses at the beginning of the next year but he did not stand a prayer. He went to every counselor at the school but I had already told them that if they touched it I would personally kill them. We held him in those courses and I guess that what happened was he got interested in them and quit trying to get out. Of course, his mother was the main reason he stayed in them. She refused to O.K his drop-add form.

He ran for president of his junior class and won! He played varsity football, and ended up being pretty good. He played the position that you run out and catch a pass. He was tall and fast and we had a good team all three of those years. His grades kept getting better and better. His senior year he ran for president of the student body and won. His first visit to me his senior year was a very eventful one for me. I told him we were going to apply for him to Annapolis and that would cover his desire to see the world. He told me that he knew that I had changed his schedule so long ago and he thanked me. He got his appointment, he was accepted, and he went. A free education, free travel and the world lay at the feet of a maid's son who had never finished the eighth grade.

He came back to speak to our graduating class when he was a senior at Annapolis and you have never seen a more handsome young man. The change in him was unbelievable. He was self confident, proud, well-spoken, looked fantastic in his uniform and what a beautiful role model he was for all the students who said you were not supposed to make good grades or to study. I wonder where he is now but I feel sure that wherever he is he is probably an Admiral. I think that I will look him up. You could if I would tell you his name but I cannot tell you that.

Now Verdell was a true success story like most of you like to hear, but what is success? You have to take into account where a student starts. I can best describe what I mean by an incident that happened to me just yesterday.

I was eating in a local restaurant with a friend of mine when the waitress looked at me and said, "I remember you, you were my senior counselor in high school and I owe my success in life all to you."

"Why thank you so much," I said, "and what are you doing now?"

"I work part time here waiting tables, and the other days I clean up a local doctor's office after the office closes. My baby and I are doing fine and I just bought my first car." Now I know that her success may not seem very big to you but for her it was a giant step. She was the only one in her family that ever graduated from high school. She was the only one in her family who existed off welfare. She was the only one in her family who had ever held down a job. See, it depends on where you start. Does it all sound gloomy to you? Well it is not. Some of these children are probably the happiest children that you will ever meet and it has nothing to do with money.

One of my main jobs as a high school counselor was to see that the students got through high school. That job was very difficult. You have seen some of the pitfalls for them already in this book. Students who might have problems were identified at an early age. This was done by teachers who cared and recognized students who were economically or socially disadvantaged, handicapped, wards of the state, abandoned by parents, truant, emotionally scarred, and hundreds of other deterrents that would cause a student to fail in the public school system. My job was to clear the way and run interference for them. To pick up that identified student and drag him, kicking and screaming, into a world that he could be productive. I did not want him armed with my middle class values. Most of them would never live in a middle class world but they could be productive and happy citizens in their world. I guess that's what this book is all about. When I started writing it, I thought that it was about the pitfalls but it is not. It is about the student's life, the successes and the failures that they experience as they move from one stage to another and the help that we try to give along the way. Maybe that's why I chose the title that I did. This book does not intend to paint anything but real life and to a lot of people, real life is sad. Strong wings are not grown by everybody but we all reach some level that enables us to fly.

The public school system has an almost insurmountable job. I have never seen a school system that did not have in its goals and objectives the words, 'Our goal is to prepare young people to develop to their fullest potential, to prepare them for the world of work and to ensure that they graduate socially adjusted.' What in the hell does that mean? I have no idea, perhaps you do. How can you measure that? How do we know that the school system is meeting its goal?

I remember one year, at graduation time, the principal and I met with an irate father who was threatening to sue the school system. He said that we were giving his son a diploma and we had not taught his son to read. He was right. We had not. The son was an EMH, or mentally handicapped, and he would never learn to read. Should the school have given him a diploma? Perhaps not. However, the goal of the school was some nebulous thing like 'help them develop to their fullest potential'. Maybe we had done that. The boy would never read or write. Perhaps the goal of the high school should be to teach a student to read and write to the best of their ability. Now that's a goal.....I could sit here and dream up those 'pie in the sky' goals forever but none of them have any meaning. You can't measure them so how can one be accountable. Perhaps we should have different goals for each student. How would that be?

Damn computers! I typed about ten pages before I went to lunch and when I came back, gone. I saved them too, two ways, I know better than to leave it just sitting there.

Anyway, I was trying to tell you about Mark. I first met him when a teacher sent him down to me to change his class for her. She said that the class he was in was too easy for him and he was causing problems in the classroom. He was agreeable so we changed his schedule. It was at the beginning of the school year and it was not too late for him to catch up in the new class. We sat and talked for a while about what he was going to do when he graduated. Going to college of course! That was the stock answer for all of them. It did not matter what courses they had taken or how hard they had worked, going to college was their answer.

The money was there for them to go but they all said that no one had told them they had to take certain courses to get in. Well that was a lie because I went to the eighth grade classes when it came time to register to tell them about what they should take and what the schools required and so forth. Do you know who tells them what to take and writes it on their registration sheet? The eighth grade teachers, that's who.

Now what do you think that teacher is going to tell a student she doesn't like. I mean one who causes her trouble in class, one who stares out the window all of the time, one who does not bring in their homework? She will not put that student in a hard curriculum; I can tell you that. That is the reason that it is so important for the parents to be involved. They need to be held accountable for their children.

The administration says, 'Oh we have our backs covered, they have to take it home for the parents to sign.' About 35% of the parents never completed the eighth grade and they are supposed to know what that student should take? I don't think so! In fact, most of the time the student signs the registration sheet themselves. This is what makes the ninth grade counselor's job so important, and most of them do not measure up to the task. They want to do group counseling for heavens sake, group counseling, as if every student in that classroom is alike. They need to talk with every ninth grade student individually, with grades and test scores in hand and place him where he needs to be even with directive counseling if necessary. They could set up appointments in the summer and have them all ready when school starts. That is too logical; is it not?

Here I am on my soapbox again and I was telling you about Mark. Mark's grandmother was what we call in the South a dry nurse. That is opposed to a wet nurse. A wet nurse lets any newborn nurse at her bosom when the mother's milk dries up. A dry nurse works for about a week to let the mother rest after delivery and get accustomed to the baby. She sleeps in the nursery with the baby and gets up in the night with them. She had been a nurse to almost every baby who had been born in this town for the past forty years. I hate to tell you this but she was even a nurse for my mother when I was born. However, I digress one more time, back to Mark. I talked with him a lot that first semester. He knew when I ate lunch, and where, and he always seemed to be around during that time. We talked about life, his grandmother, his mother, his plans, his teachers, anything that might be helpful to him or that which I could help him. I liked him.

One Monday morning when we came to school, we discovered that someone had broken in over the weekend and vandalized the school. They had stolen some computers, projectors, and the money out of the vending machines. It was pretty bad.

Late that afternoon, I discovered that Mark had been arrested, as one of three boys who the police thought was responsible. That was not possible!

The District Attorney was a very good friend of mine and I called him that night. I was indignant. I had never heard of racial profiling at that time, but I felt like that was what the police had done; picked up the first black boy they had found on the street. On and on I went. I even think I said that if they did not let him go, I would sue them for libel. Boy was I stupid! He listened to me rant and rave forever and when I stopped to take a breath he quietly said, "Now calm down, I hate to tell you this but he confessed." I know that you have heard the saying 'took the wind out of my sails.' Well, mine were luffing so badly that I needed to take them down. I could hardly get my breath.

That night I went up to see Mark in the jail. "I didn't do it, I didn't do it," he said. "The police frightened me so bad that I just told them I did to get them off my back. I was with the boys earlier but I left them and went home before they broke in the schools. You have got to help me." We had Legal Aid Service in the town at that time and they defended Mark. The kicker was that the other two boys swore that he was with them and what was the jury to think after the confession and the testimony of the other two boys.

I think of Mark often. I wonder if he really did it. Somehow, I feel that he was innocent and that makes me feel guilty. I am still good friends with the District Attorney and we still talk about Mark now and then.

He tells me that I am a patsy and a Pollyanna. I had rather be that than sitting judgment on young people when there is always a trace of doubt. I don't remember what the sentencing was, but I do think that he served time and I know that he never came back to school. His grandmother died not long after that and I went to the funeral but he was not there.

Jane's father owned a couple of strip malls in town and a huge construction company. She was pretty in a strange sort of way. Perhaps we should call her interesting, not pretty. She was a little on the pudgy side with flaming red hair and freckles. She was very likable. When she came to see me, she would always talk about how liberal her parents were. They loved to have her friends go places with them regardless of race color or creed, and to have her house always full of all kinds of people. She explained how understanding her parents were. She was a little bit of a know-it-all if you know what that means, but I still liked her. I never saw her talking with anybody in school or eating with anyone. She seemed to be pretty much of a loner to me. She had been accepted at a state supported college not too far from our town and planned to major in Journalism. She wanted to work for a newspaper. She had worked for the high school paper and had written some pretty good articles.

She started coming more and more often and I knew that I was going to have to put a stop to it because I had to leave off some of this crisis counseling and get on with the preventive counseling. Somehow, I had to hit on the right question to ask her to find out what the trouble was. I knew that there was trouble. "Are you pregnant," I asked her one day right out of the blue. The shock treatment usually works best in a situation like this.

"Yes," she answered. "My Mother and Daddy have told me that I have to have it and after it is born I will have to give it up for adoption. However, I will not do it and I told them so. Why do you think that they are making me have it? I don't want it. They think that they can order me around but I will show them. This is my baby and I will keep it." Her red hair was showing.

"What about college?" I asked.

"Of course I am still going. I will just have to hire someone to keep the baby."

"What about the money to do that?" I asked. She sputtered around for a while and ending up saying that her parents would just have to pay for it.

She had the baby! It was black. The father told her that he would not pay for her school and the last that I heard, she was working at Wall-Mart trying to save up enough money to go to school. What a waste! I never had a private session with her again so I don't know what happened between her and her parents. I can only guess that she stood her ground, kept the baby, while they stood theirs and would not help her with the money. What a horrible way to have to learn a lesson. As I told you before, when young people make a mistake, it could affect them for the rest of their lives.

I made so many mistakes during those years. I am sure that every counselor does when first starting out in the public school system. Most of my mistakes were rectifiable and did not end up hurting anyone permanently, but I know that they caused some traumatic times for young people and I am very sorry for that. Some of my worst mistakes involved a wonderful judge who sat on the domestic bench.

Sometimes the words flow out of your mind through your fingers and on to the page in what seems like a never-ending stream. You don't want to sleep, you don't want to eat, and you don't want to get up from your chair. Other times, the words dry up like my grass when it has not rained for two months in the summer and you just sit and stare at the blank page. I wonder why that happens. I have heard people talk about creative juices but that does not mean anything to me. They are just idle words with no scientific basis. I have been on page 131 for about three weeks now. It is not that I do not have a world more to tell, my head is full. It is just that the words will not come out.

However, back to the judge. I thought that I could move mountains, the enabler I called myself! I knew that I could do more behind the scenes than out front so I called this judge that I knew would be sitting on the child support cases of some of my high school students and asked to meet with him in chambers. I would get to tell him what I thought should be done with the students before the Child Support Services got to him in court because I thought that I knew more about the student than they did. It never dawned on me that some of the students might not be telling me all of the truth.

When I think back on those days, I always smile. I smile as I remember the judge and his office and my earnest pleading for my students. He must have smiled too at this stupid, intense white girl who thought that she knew all of the answers. In her pretty, high heeled shoes. He never laughed at me, he never failed to do what I asked; he never failed to see me when I called and that seems so strange when I think of some of the outcomes. Perhaps in his infinite wisdom, he realized that there was no answer. There was no right and wrong way. The only thing that you could do was to try something and if that didn't work, try something else.

His office looked like it came right out of a TV show. It was about the size of a postage stamp. In there, books, papers, cigarettes, ashtrays (full), even clothes were strewn everywhere. It had one huge desk that almost took up the whole room with a big, big chair behind it and a big wingback chair in front of the desk for his visitors. When sitting, the visitor's knees touched the wall. You could not take more than three steps in any direction without bumping into the walls. I am not even sure that he had a secretary. The county, the courthouse, the Social Services system, all were one horse back then; you know, country. Now the man that sat behind that desk was a different matter. He was tall, stately, thin, drop-dead good looking, and probably in his sixty's. I spent five years in that wingback chair talking to him about students that I wanted him to help and I enjoyed every minute of it. One of the first cases that I took to him was Julie.

Julie was a freshman, just turned fifteen and was still under the jurisdiction of Social Services, barely. When she first came into my office, she was crying. A teacher had brought her down to me. The tale that she told me was beyond my imagination (do not forget this middle class background that I was saddled with). She lived in a trailer with her mother and father, two older brothers and a younger sister. There were two bedrooms in the trailer. I gathered from what she said that her father was an alcoholic. When he received his paycheck on Friday, he would come home drunk as a lord, hollering, swearing and would end up beating her mother and her senseless. This happened every Friday. She was a waif of a child, with big circles under her eyes, and long stringy hair that looked like it had never been washed and her clothes were dirty. I asked her if he ever beat the younger sister and she said no but that she knew that her time would come soon and she wanted them both to get out of there before he started. She never said but I guessed that her brothers abused her too, probably sexually. Psychology has only scratched the tip of the iceberg when it comes to sibling abuse. She said that her mom didn't work and she couldn't leave because she didn't have anywhere to go. Julia said that she had tried and tried to talk her mother into getting out, to no avail. She pleaded with me to help her before her father killed her.

I talked to her about four times after that and I took her home one day after school. I promise you, that trailer was about thirty feet long, rusted out, dirty, front screen hanging off, and a well in the yard. Nobody should have had to live in that and five people did. I talked to her mother for a long time. I explained to her about Harbor House. It is called different things in different towns but it is a halfway house for women who are abused. It is somewhere for them to stay until they get on their feet again and can find a job. She was not receptive. It fact she was non-committal. She even seemed apathetic about her children. It was almost as if she was on drugs but she could not have been because she could not have paid for them.

Hell flew into me and I wanted those two girls out of that house right then. I went straight to the judge's office. We talked for an hour about the situation and then I reported the abuse to Social Services. They went out the next day, removed the two girls from the home, and placed them in foster care. Good foster care! I knew the people that took them in. I talked to the older girl quite a bit for the next month or so and once I felt as though she was settled I tapered the counseling off a little bit. It was about three months after we removed her that she came in my office one day and told me that she wanted to go back to her mother and daddy and that her younger sister did too. Can you believe that? At that time, I could not believe that she would want to go back to the beatings, the incest, and the drinking. But, it didn't take me many years to figure out that no matter how bad things get, or how much abuse gets dealt out, children still love their parents and they want to be with them.

She tried to explain to me how she felt but it was beyond my understanding. We moved her back home. She had one little paper sack of belongings so it was easy. I don't even think she had a dress to her name. How much stuff would you have to pack to move one of your children? I cried when I saw her go back into that house with her one little paper sack. I saw her mother and daddy hug both of the girls. I couldn't see to drive home for the tears. I thought about how much we take for granted and how little we realize what is going on the world around us.

I would like to be able to tell you that I have seen Julia since she graduated and that all is well with her but I have not seen her. I do not know what happened to her but I do know that she had very little chance of a different kind of life and my heart is heavy when I think of all of the children like her and how they keep in the rut because it is so deep.

Not all of the cases were like Julie's and I am sure that the younger children fared better when you removed them from the home but once they got into high school, there were very few exceptions, they wanted to go home. I guess the longer you live in the home the better equipped you are to handle what the parents dish out and I guess that you are physically stronger too and that helps. I know that with the boys it does because they tell daddy they will beat the hell out of him if he doesn't leave them alone. I know that you have read of all of the cases that sons keep mothers safe from drunken husbands and a lot of times they kill the father if he does not leave her alone.

Another judge case was Dorothy. Dorothy lived with her mother and two younger sisters. No father was on the scene and the mother had nightly visitors, most of them were paying visitors. The first time that Dorothy came to see me it was not about her home life. She wanted to talk about one of her teachers. Somehow we got around to her mother and then to her mother's friends. She said that the men had started making passes at her and one of them had tried to get into bed with her after he had finished with her mother. This horrified her and she ran out of the house and spent the night in the car with the doors locked. She was fifteen at the time. It was not until she told me that her mother had approached her to help her out with the household bills by taking in a few men that I went into action. 'Miss Goody Two Shoes', that's me.

"You can't live in that house any longer", I told her, "and we need to think about your two younger sisters too." We went through the sexually transmitted disease bit, and the pregnancy bit and the AIDS bit and all of those other bits. I went into the decision-making mode and promoted open discussion on the pros and cons of early sexual activity and the implications for the adolescent's future family, career, and life plans.

"It's no big deal," she said to me. "I can make a little money that way and maybe buy a car. It is not as if I have to love the man. Just screw him."

I know that by now you are thinking that this is something that I read in a cheap novel. Well, I am here to tell you that it is life, it is real, and she meant every word that she was saying to me. What in the hell difference did it make in the scheme of things was her attitude! I think at this point, I really talked her into letting me tell Social Services so that I could get all three of them out of that house. I told myself that maybe somehow I could make a difference in her life. I told her all of the good things about getting out of the house and none of the bad. I told her that her sisters would have it better than she had it. I told her that if she waited until she was sixteen, there was nothing that I could do for her.

To the Judge I went and we mapped out our strategy and a day later we were in court with Social Services and all three girls were moved into a foster home. I do not even remember the ages of the other two girls but I do remember that they were younger. Do you know how long they stayed there? You guessed it, about six months. After this case, I went to talk to the Judge and I told him that I would never meet in his office with him again. That was the end of my being an enabler in that sense of the word.

I promised myself that I would leave that kind of work to Social Services and only counsel the students and report what they would allow in Social Services. It wasn't too long after that though before we were made to report everything to them and what a mess that was. During those years, I had a sign in my office that read 'Do not tell me anything that you do not want Social Services to hear. That is especially true if it has anything to do with child abuse'. It did not stop them. It was as if they had to tell somebody, anybody. The words just had to come out.

I saw Dorothy about ten years later. She made it out of her trailer. She had taken a course at the local community college and was working as a paralegal for a local lawyer, making damn good money too. I did not ask her how she got the money to move out and go to school but I thought that I knew. She thanked me repeatedly for all the help that I had given her. Here again I wondered, what help. However, I think that I knew. I listened to her, I put some ideas in her head and I let her know that someone cared.

I see parents today pushing their children from one thing to another: soccer, football, swim team, two sports at one time, all kinds of meetings and it makes me tired. I wonder when the children get to kick the can or smell the roses or be a kid, or talk to someone about growing up. Parents even do it at school. They move heaven and earth to get their children in this class or that class or this program or that program. Sometimes they are demanding that their children be placed where they cannot succeed, where they cannot develop the self-confidence or the self-esteem that they will need for the rest of their life. I believe that parents should be involved, always, but they must also be realistic about their children's abilities. This is very hard for parents. Even when test scores are staring them in the face and the people who are talking with them know what they are talking about, they still will demand something above their child's ability.

I wasn't one of my principal's favorite people all of the time because there were so many times that we just didn't see eye to eye and I never hesitated telling him so. He would blow up, just get furious, and even scream at me but then it was all over and most of the time I got what I wanted. Not all of the time though and there were times that I knew better than crossing him. He ran a good ship and it was tough back in those days to hold things together. Most of it was by the seat of your pants. We got into trouble mainly with problems that he involved me in concerning the faculty.

Take for instance the time that his black assistant principal was accused of sexual harassment. Now, back in those days, I didn't even know what the words meant and I remember very vividly going back to my office and looking them up in the dictionary. Harassment means to, 1. to worry or torment 2. to trouble by repeated raids or attacks. Since sexual is an adjective, I guess that he was worrying them sexually. What! I knew that man pretty good and he had never worried or attacked me sexually. Both of those teachers were young, I mean young. When I talked with the two teachers who were accusing him, they said that he was putting his arms around them and talking close. Talking close! What does that mean? I tried to tell them that it was his way of belonging, being chummy, being white. However, they would have none of that and the next thing that I knew one of the secretaries had gotten in on it and they were filling out papers on him. The principal let two teachers and a secretary ruin that man's career.

Then, papers went in to the county office. They all descended on our school with their lawyers and he was whisked away, never to be seen again while the principal did not lift a finger. He never said, 'Let me keep him until due process is carried out, I don't believe he is guilty'. He said nothing and his comment to me was, "Well you know that you have to back up your teachers." Back up your teachers, my fanny. That man was one of his teachers. When I told him that his problem was that he was afraid of rocking the boat, he blew his stack. I thought he was going to throw me out of his office but he didn't.

Then there was the time that he asked me to observe one of his teacher's classes. She had slapped a black girl and the girl had gone to the principal and told him that the teacher was picking on her in class too and she thought that the teacher was a racist. Back in those days, you could get by with hitting a black student once. Especially if they mouthed off at you. Anyway, I was stupid enough to go and what made it even worse was that I wrote up my observation. I never understood why I felt that I had to put it on paper.

What I had to say about her was not the kindest thing that I have ever said about someone. There were some other issues that I had with her besides her classroom and I put those on paper too. They dealt with race also, like nominations for this and that or selecting students to represent things. She never chose a black for anything. I put that in my report also. He called me down to talk with me about 'the report' and there she sat. She had my report to him in her hand. Can you imagine! He gave it to her to read. I forgot to tell you, her husband and her son were lawyers and when I came in, she jumped up and said to me, "I will see you in court, this report is slanderous." Chalk one up for inexperience. That was the last time that I ever wrote a report on anyone in that school on paper.

Carrying me to court never materialized. Cooler heads prevailed. Nevertheless, for about a month there I was very nervous. I did not even acknowledge my principal for about a month. I would pass him on the hall and turn my head the other way. Like he cared!

About five years later, he apologized to me, after a fashion, but by that time, it really did not matter. I had moved on with my life. It had taken about ten years for me to understand how he would react and he finally figured out that I would always take the student's side so we managed to compromise and our working relationship turned out to be pretty good. I would write all of his recommendations for him. I would leave them on his desk and he would sign them, take the credit for them, and he was happy. Any time an irate parent came to see him the secretary had been instructed to call me down first and let me calm them down and he would come strolling in and say that he had been in a meeting. Well, I was better than he was at that anyway.

I cannot remember all of the details about Sam but I hope that I get most of them right when I tell you about him. However, don't do research on the Atlantic Coast Conference regulations because I am telling you up front I may have something about it wrong. Sam was a hell-of-a football player. The high school was 4A in those days and we played football with the big boys. All of the college coaches were looking at him from his sophomore year on. The only problem with him was his grades, bad!! He could run with that football though.

Now Sam had never been out of the county that he lived in. Probably, he never been out of the town that he lived in, but I am not sure about the town. His mother was on welfare and the coach took him home every day after practice because he did not have a ride. He was a sweet boy and he tried hard, he just didn't have it when it came to books. He was so excited about maybe getting to play college ball that he could not stand it. I think that what he was really excited about too was maybe being able to see a little bit of the outside world. I kept telling him that he had to end up with a C average or the colleges wouldn't be able to sign him. This was before the days of the new regulations, you know, an 800 SAT, core college courses, and all of that stuff.

I have heard all of the arguments about graduation rates for college athletics. I have heard the outcry about coach abuse of players. Let me tell you about the other side of the story. That kid gets to see a life outside of welfare, outside of one shanty on a dirt road, outside of sharing a mattress on the floor with three other siblings. In addition, I do not care if he graduates from college or not because he is so much better off than he was before he got there. A college degree for a kid like that is not the most important thing in the world and do not let anybody fool you. You can get a kid all of the financial aid in the world but somehow he has to get bus fare to get there. Middle class folks do not understand that. Anyway, back to Sam.

He would sit in my office and tell me all the things that he was going to do. How after four years he would sign with the pros, make a lot of money, and move his mother somewhere that was better than where she was. He would buy a car and not have to depend on someone carrying him everywhere. Most of what he would do was simple things, things that you and I take for granted. He had never seen a building over three stories high; he had never ridden a train, or a plane. He had never eaten in a restaurant or slept in a room by himself. He had never had a suit of clothes or a dress jacket, as he called it, and he had never had a new pair of jeans.

Graduation time came and he failed the math that he needed to graduate by one point. One Point! I had been keeping up with his grades and I knew that they were very shaky but I really did not expect him to fail. I went to my principal and we decided that I would go to the math teacher and see if I could talk her into changing his grade and passing him. The big problem was that he could not get it in summer school because no buses ran and he did not have a way to get there. No car in the family, remember.

The principal said, "Go talk to her, and if the witch won't change the grade, I will."

I begged, I pleaded, I told her all about Sam and everything that could be his if she would just pass him. She would not budge, no sir. "He has to learn his lesson," she said. "He didn't turn in all of his homework." Moreover, in her mind he exhibited complete disregard for her course. All he could think about was football and being a big man on campus. I got to thinking about if Sam even had electricity in his house to do his homework and promised myself that I would check that out. He probably copied all of his buddies' homework when he got to school. That was what most of the jocks did.

I know that you are going to cringe when I say this, but the principal changed his grade from a 69 to a 70 and off Sam went to college. He stayed in college two years and was drafted by the Redskins. He became a major player for them for about ten years. He got his car, his mother's new house, and a bedroom all to himself. Now I ask you, was it important that he got a degree from college? Was it important that he graduated from college? He is not on welfare. He is not living at the end of that dirt road with no electricity. Your tax dollars are not going to raise his children. He broke that chain!

The math teacher pranced her butt to the principal's office the next year and wanted to know where Sam was. She had heard that he had gone to college and she told the principal that I had changed his grade in her class so that he could graduate. When the principal told her to get out of his office, she went to the county office and tried to cause trouble for the principal. We weathered that storm but she had a big mouth and she ran it for a long time.

While we are on football, I must tell you about the time that the whole football team resigned at Monday practice after the first big game of the season. When I came to work on Tuesday morning every player was siting in the guidance office waiting for me. Now I am sure that you are asking what a counselor has to do with a football team. I was asking myself the same question. It took quite a while to piece it all together but it turned out that the coach was verbally abusing them at the game, screaming at them, sending some of the best players to the locker room for the rest of the game because of what he called stupid playing. He was cussing them out in front of the opposing team. This had been going on at practice ever since it started and I guess that the game was just the culmination of it all. I have told you before that coaches ran the school system in those days. Principals were ex-coaches and the coach was king of the campus. I could not in my wildest imagination think of what a coach could do without a team, cancel the rest of the football games, resign because he had nothing to do, pick a new team? None of these sounded plausible so I felt that I would go and talk with him about the situation. I got nowhere as you can imagine. Then I talked the principal into having a meeting with all of the players, the coach, the principal, and myself.

We met in the auditorium and the coach got on the stage and started in on the players. He called them every vile word that he could think of. Things like patsies, wimps, pussies, little boys hiding under skirts. On and on he went with the most degrading talk that I have ever heard. Suddenly it dawned on me why the team had come to me and what my role was. I stood up and waited for him to take a breath. It took a long time but it finally came and I said, "These boys do not have to put up with your garbage talk any longer. We are leaving this meeting and I am calling each one of their parents. We will meet you in court. You are slandering them and I will not put up with it." That afternoon the principal moved the assistant principal to head coach and the ex head coach went to an institution where he received physiological help for the next four months. That team won the 4A state championship that year. They were not all that good but what they lacked in talent, they made up in courage and perseverance. The coach came back the following year and some of the same boys played for him. He was still there when I left thirty years later.

I can't believe that this stupid computer lost about three pages of my stuff while I was at lunch. I saved it too before I left. It was the hardest part that I have written because I was trying to tell you what counselors do again. When I thought over what I had written, I was not sure that

I explained it very well. I was hoping that I had not left the impression that we are straws in the wind and just go in any direction that the wind blows. We are not straws and we always have a plan. It changes depending on each child's situation, race, and background. The plan does not always work and sometimes, more often than not, the results are not what we planned. The one thing that you must remember, we always have the student's best interest at heart.

I think that one of the reasons that I made a good counselor was that I really liked young people. In addition, I was very careful to set the stage so that students did not feel that I was an authority figure. I never sat at my desk with a student in my 30 years of counseling (I know that I have said that before). I had a round table in my office with two chairs, a lamp and a messy top, always messy with all of the paper work that counselors have to do. I never tried to sit taller than they did and I would even lean over to achieve this some time, especially when it was really difficult for the student to get his story out. I did all of this because I wanted the student to feel that he was with an accepting person in an accepting place. That I was empathetic, genuine and not judgmental was important if I was to help the student with any developmental deficits that they might have.

Children have traumatic things that occur in their lives that cause deficits. When their physical and psychological needs are not met because of these traumatic events, they have 'gaps' in their development that require help. Some of these traumas could be divorce, parental death, or even abusive parenting practices. They also occur when young people have to face crisis situations that they are not equipped to handle such as social pressure from drugs, or sexual situations like intercourse, abortion, or sexually transmitted diseases. Wilson and Mason (1990) have even developed a model for treating these adolescents. This is not the only method that is used but it has been very effective for me. The goal is to identify the student's unmet needs and facilitate developmental growth so that the student will be more mature in their levels of functioning. Most counselors try to fill in the gaps that the student failed to learn in their development (Ann Vernon 1993, *Counseling Children and Adolescents*, Love Publishing Company). I did not want to talk about all of this and it makes me tired and you bored I know, but I felt that I owed you a small explanation of method.

I have a friend whom I love to talk with because of the freshness of her thoughts. I will describe her to you by saying that she wears blue jeans with holes in the knees to school, she is a teacher, and when they tell her she cannot come to school that way, she says, "Fuck the establishment." She is that good and how lucky the young people are to have her teach them. Anyway, she says that counselors wear all kinds of hats, but the main one is the hat that says, "Oh everything is wonderful, the teachers are wonderful, the school is wonderful, the classes are wonderful, the principal is wonderful, wonderful, wonderful … and on and on…"

Can't you see our white teeth and our plastic smiles? Whom do we think we are kidding? Surely not the parent, maybe we ourselves come to mind. We sit in our lofty seats and dispense this information when we know damn well we are lying through our teeth. Our salvation? We love kids. We care. We protect them with our very lives … and God help anybody who mucks with them.

CHAPTER 21

Another New Principal

And then I got a new principal, and what a principal he was! He was tall, thin, young, manic-depressive, medicated, and charged with new ideas. I have never seen a man quite so driven. He charged through the school like a whirlwind dragging everyone in his wake. He was not a curriculum man; he left that to his teachers. How wonderful because they were all good. He wanted everything to be a show. I really felt that he probably had quite a few 'gaps' in his development but we will not go there.

He was a showman in every sense of the word. The first thing that he did was to take the attendance room next to his office for a meeting place. He changed all of the counter tops to something that looked like dark green marble. He changed all of the carpet to dark green to match the marble. Do you have any idea how dark green carpet looked after one thousand students marched across it each day? You get the idea. The janitor was really pissed off. It ended up being a beautiful conference room but I will tell you all about it later.

He was the first principal that I ever knew that was not a coach. I do not know where he got all of the money to make the changes but it probably came out of school supply money or the athletic fund. I would bet on the athletic fund because he did not care anything about athletics. I know that the coaches had a hard time while he was there. I really felt that by the middle of the second semester we would be out of paper to run work off for the students.

This might be a really good place to tell you about the records. All schools have to keep all of the records of every student who ever went to that school so they can furnish transcripts for whatever the student wants to do for the rest of their lives. Well, you can imagine how many records could accumulate over the years as classes graduated from a school. By this time, our school had been running for about twenty years and we graduated about 365 every year so we had about 7,300 records in storage. He moved all of those records six times before he left. Each time he would put them somewhere, he would change his mind and make that room something else with curtains and chairs and furniture and so on. I thought before it was all over we would move the records outside. He was not interested in them anyway. The final resting place was the guidance department and he built a vault for them there about the size of a postage stamp and put the filing cabinets on top of each other so that the counselors had to have ladders to get to them. He did not have any old counselors, I can tell you that because they could not climb the ladders.

One of the things that describe him best was that he liked to 'do' weddings. I guess you would call him a wedding planner. I went to a wedding that he did one time and everything about the wedding was black. The bridesmaids dresses, the flowers, the nosegays, the roll out carpet, the works. Now I am not against black night weddings but this wedding was at 2:00 in the afternoon and all that sunshine made everything look really bad.

It is tough to break in a new principal, especially when he is moving all of the time and everything that I would try to tell or ask him he would say, "You make the decision". Then, off he would go to change something else about the physical building, like curtains for the lunchroom. He had his portrait painted and hung it in the front hall. He had breakfast in the library for all of the business leaders in the community. Now that was a good idea but let me tell you it was a bunch of work. He wanted all of the best China plates, silver, centerpiece, crystal, silver-serving dishes, and linen table clothes were all necessary to put on the show. We were carting and carrying for a month to put that on. He served about 75 at each breakfast and the home economics teacher and I did all the work. Now I ask you, can you find that in the job description of a guidance counselor? We also had all of the student leaders there, president of all of the classes, president of the National Honor Society, president of this and that. That was a good idea. A lot of publicity came from those who came for breakfast and a lot of good will came from the community. He was a master at that. He set the stage for all of the rest that he asked for.

He did not have time for the students. He would pick out four or five boys and they would be his pets. He would call them down for everything that he wanted done and they could get by with anything that they wanted to do. They were not academic students, just your average everyday kid. Some responded positively to his attention and others, well they were not so happy about being singled out. They said it made them feel queer! They would almost run from him when they saw him coming. He never seemed to understand that they did not want his favors bestowed on them. He was married with no children but there was still something about him. … I think that he felt very uncomfortable with the very bright students who were leaders in the class. I need to set the record straight right here; I liked him. I liked working for him. I liked his style and he was effective.

He had been a middle school principal, you know sixth, seventh and eighth grades and he brought some of the ideas that he used there with him to high school. One of those ideas was that all of a grade was to take a trip to Washington for a weekend. He bestowed this privilege on the ninth grade class. You would have thought that he had given them a million dollars. The seniors always took a trip but ninth graders never got to go anywhere. You have already guessed it; I was elected to go. They could not get enough chaperones and at the last minute, one that they had corralled had to drop out so then there was me. He promised me that I would not have to go on the senior trip that year so away I went. My experience with ninth graders had been zero except for my two girls when they whizzed through that age. I am here to tell you they are nothing like seniors. When that Greyhound bus pulled out with what seemed like 100 students, I knew that I was in for the ride of my life.

That first night in the hotel, I learned a great many things. You have to have a security guard on the halls after lights out at all times. This is to keep the boys and girls from commingling. A trashcan must be placed against an open door to the hotel rooms to hold the door open until lights out. Strange isn't it? You learn to do the electric slide in the hall, regardless of your age. You must have room-check every thirty minutes. You cannot, under any circumstances, go to sleep unless you are able to wake up every thirty minutes to do your room check. It is unbelievable, even with this close supervision that you can still find boys in girls' rooms and girls in boys' rooms. How do they get there without anyone seeing them? It is beyond me. I realized that in spite of this, I was really having a great time and the kids were wonderful.

The next day the touring was fantastic. The bus pulled right up to where ever we were going, we got out, and when we got through there it was sitting right there waiting for us. No walking! That night, we had a moonlight dinner cruise on the Potomac with a band and dancing until twelve. There were other ninth grade classes on board. One of them I remember very well was from California.

The next day, we hit the Smithsonian. I think that it was the science building because I looked up and saw the dinosaur right after the girl screamed, "There they are!" One of the men ran over to our group and talked for a long time to the Principal. He motioned for me to come over and the story went something like this. When the students were going up the steps and out of the boat the night before, one of our precious boys had run his hand up one of the girls' dress from California. It seems that his hand went inside her pants and found its mark. I remember seeing this particular girl on the dance floor and the skirt that she had on barely covered her 'Lucy', as my mother used to call it, and I also remembered that her 'Lucy' was shaking real good when I saw it on the dance floor. Now I am not saying that she was asking for it, but the thought did come to my mind when this man was so outraged. The Principal looked like he had forgotten to take his medicine that morning and he also seemed to have lost his voice.

I spoke up and said, "Now just what is it that you want us to do about this?"

The man stammered, hemmed, hawed, and finally said, "The least that he can do is apologize to her."

This seemed futile to me but the Principal found his voice and said. "Of course, and you can rest assured that he will be punished when he gets back home and to school and his parents will be told about this also." By this time, he was hyperventilating so badly that I thought he would faint.

The boy was brought out in front of the group, the girl was brought out in front of the group, and he apologized with a flourish. If he thought that it was the end of it, he was in for a surprise. The principal verbally abused him for an hour and called him everything he could think of that was fit for ninth grade ears. He told him things like "You have broken my faith and trust in you; you are lower than any scum that I have ever been off with. I will never take you anywhere again. "She," he pointed at me, "will tell your parents and they will punish you also", on and on he went. I knew that I would get the raw end of that deal. After his tirade was over, the adults went in to have some coffee and the kids did a little shopping. He still could not stop talking about it and I thought he was going to have a heart attack.

I finally said, "Get a life. This is not the end of the world. You have run this into the ground long enough and nobody wants to hear it anymore. I am going to do some shopping too because I don't want to hear you talk about it anymore." His mouth flew open in surprise but that was the end of it for a while.

That night I got the boy aside and did a little counseling. I told him that it was not the end of the world and he had to go on from here. Maybe he had learned something from it, or I hoped so, and that sort of stuff. I did not want him to be completely crushed. I also told him that I did not think less of him because of it. I conveniently forgot to tell his parents when we got home. I knew that the principal would not tell them. The boy had suffered enough.

I saw him a lot over the next three years. I guess that I became his personal counselor even though he was not a senior. In fact, all of those ninth graders that went on the trip beat a steady path to my office door for every little thing. It was nice to grow up with them. I always thought that a counselor should move up with her students. You end up knowing them so much better but we had so many bad counselors during those years that no student should have to put up with some of them for four years.

As I told you before, the new principal turned the workroom at the school into a conference room. Dark green faux pas marble and I mean what I said, because it was a social blunder. The green marble-looking linoleum covered the counter tops and half of the wall. He installed dark green carpet to match the green faux pas marble linoleum. He put a phone in the room, it was green, and a beautiful pecan conference table with eight chairs and that is where he met with his teachers, parents, and me. He always met with his students in his office; they were never invited to come to this room. He kept a large coffeepot and green mugs there. Every day the lunchroom would bring in cookies, or whatever was sweet on the menu for the day, in for his guests. The idea was great, I'm not knocking that. The parents loved it but it could have been made a little less showy. It was interesting to see how the parents reacted in the room that they thought was so fine. They were always on their best behavior, the word got around, and they started coming a little dressed up because they had heard about the room. No one had been to a room like that in a school. Not from this poor county anyway. They were always polite and easy to deal with in there. Now isn't that interesting? A lot could be learned from that but that's another story.

He got the PTA to bring in stuff in the mornings for the teachers to eat before school started. That was kind of like a little breakfast, and the teachers loved it. They felt like somebody cared and it started their day off on a good foot. See how something simple like that can set the tone of a school. In the end, the students were the ones who benefited in a roundabout way. He was a flitter though, he would flit in and flit out and leave in the middle of a conversation or meeting. It was always left for somebody else to clean up and usually it was I.

Well, I started telling you all about this room because of one teacher that we had. Her elevator did not quite go to the top floor and she was kind of out of touch with reality. Most of these odd behaviors had started fairly recently, say in the past three weeks, and the principal had become alarmed about her behavior. He sent me a note and told me that he wanted me to meet with them in 'the room' after school one day. There were just the three of us there and I think that he started the conversation off with some inane questions about how her classes were going. She looked at him and told him that he was threatening her, and she started screaming. He up and left the room on the run and left me with the screaming woman.

She started taking her clothes off and she kept telling me that she was burning up. I was trying my best to stay calm but it was very difficult to say the least. I called out and told the secretary to call the rescue squad, by now the town had one, and lock the doors to the room so that she could not get out. That left me in there with her, of course, but it was not the kind of situation that made me afraid for my life. I had had plenty of those but this was not one of them. By the time that the EMS people got there, she was completely disrobed on top of the table and I was sitting in one of the pecan chairs talking to her. She had broken all of the green cups and the cookies were crushed in the green carpet. She had overturned the coffee pot and the room was in a mess. It took almost everyone in the office to get her covered up and in the truck for the trip to Mental Health. The really bad thing was that one of the EMT's who came was one of her students who only attended school until lunch and went to work for the rescue squad during the afternoon. I know that it must have been very embarrassing for him but he never let on that he even knew her.

It turned out that she had been taking diet pills because she had put on some weight that year and they really did her in. It took the rest of the year for her to recover but she was back in the classroom the next fall. I only tell you this story to show you that there was never a dull moment in school and every day it was different. All of the books talk about counselors who end up being crisis counselors when they should be preventive counselors. It is almost next to impossible to set up a preventive program in high school. The fires have to be put out!

CHAPTER 22

The Light and Dark Hallways

It was about this time that I met Renee. I had heard about Renee long before I ever met her. I heard the teachers talking about how smart she was. They all said that she was probably one of the smartest students that they had ever taught. Her family did not have much and there were three or four children in the home. Her father was a tenant farmer; you know tended someone's tobacco for them for a percentage of the income. Everyone seemed to think that she might end up being number one in her senior class when she graduated.

I decided that I was going to see to it that she went to college. She was a junior when she first walked into my office. I started by paving the way for her. We talked about college, college and more college. We talked about majors, majors and more majors. We talked about money, how much it took, how much you made with a college degree, how much you made without one. I gave her as much encouragement as anyone could have possibly given any child of their own. I gave her books to read to stimulate her thinking, everything I could find that would encourage her and lead her in the right direction. We visited college campuses and talked to admission officers. I left no stone unturned.

Her senior year came and we filled out financial aid papers. When the time came, she was accepted at a nice state supported school that we had visited. They gave her a nice academic scholarship that covered almost all of her tuition, books and board. Financial aid came through with everything else that she needed, and she was set.

You have already guessed it, haven't you? She walked into my office one day in early spring. She sat down in my armchair and from the look on her face; I knew what was coming. "I'm sorry that I am going to let you down," she said. "But, you know that I really don't want to go to college don't you? I would be going just for you and that will not get it. Regardless of what you say, I cannot do it. I am the only one in my family who has ever graduated from high school. It will have to be my children that make the next leap to college. I know that you have done everything that you could for the past two years to make me want to go but two years cannot undo what my family has done for a lifetime. They think that I should be out working, making money, and that is all that they talk about. I would be so guilty if I went to college that I probably never would get over it. Forgive me. I am going to get married in June and he will be joining the army as soon as he graduates and I am going with him whereever they send him. I appreciate everything that you have done for me, more than you will ever know, but I just can't do it."

I felt like someone had hit me in the stomach with a sledgehammer. I could not get my breath. I knew that my approach was all wrong with her. I should have made her want to go rather than making it easy for her. I should have dwelled more on the outcomes of a college education rather than the education itself. I could think of a million things that I should have done but I could tell that none of them would work now; her mind was made up. That beautiful, intelligent child said goodbye to me that day and walked out of my life. I knew from the very beginning that I was fighting a losing battle. I knew that the influence that her parents had on her was so much greater than my influence. For her to make that break was almost impossible. What is that old saying that my Mother used, 'You can lead a horse to water but you can't make him drink?' There is a lot of truth in that.

I saw her many years later. She brought three beautiful children into my office and she was probably one of the happiest girls that I had ever seen. It was written all over her face. "These are the ones who will go to college", she told me. I knew that she was right. They had her behind them and they would grow up with a lifetime of encouragement and she would let them know that it was a given that they would attend college, no excuses. When you look at it that way, perhaps I did make a difference in her life.

I have tried to interject some light stuff in here because when you deal with troubled youth, it gets very heavy. Sometimes it is so heavy you can't take it and as you have already seen, things just don't have a happy ending. The have and the have not's, most of time, remain the have and have not's. The few that make it, keep you going. They are the silver lining. I have told you before, making it means different things to different people and sometimes we get confused because what we think is a failure turns out to be a success to those on the other side of the fence.

I saw what I thought was a failure in the grocery store yesterday. She had muscular dystrophy in high school. I mean a really bad case. She stuttered so badly that you could hardly understand what she was saying. She walked with braces on both arms and it pained you to watch her because you knew what effort that she put into each step that she took. When she talked, you really did not want to sit in front of her because she opened her mouth so wide for each word that you could almost see her tonsils. We had an elevator in the school and she had a key to go up and down. There was a mentally retarded boy in the school who was very nice looking who started carrying her books for her and I had a 'permanent late to class' pass made for him so he could get her books to her seat and still get to his class, only a little late.

She came into my office one day and after she got all settled in my chair she looked at me and said that she was in love. She was a very positive person. She went on to say that they were perfect for each other. She was very bright and he was very strong. He needed her to survive and she needed him to get along. I couldn't argue with that. However, for some reason, I felt that it was my calling to educate her on all of the pitfalls that might come with their union. We talked and talked and talked some more. They graduated that year and the next year, I heard that they had gotten married. So much for my wonderful counseling. I did not hear from them again until I saw them in the grocery store, what is this, seven years, no eight years later. He was pushing her in a wheel chair. She had a baby in her arms and there were two little children with them. I guessed that one was about six and one was probably three. I have never seen a happier family.

Are the children mentally retarded? Probably! Should they have brought them into this world for society to look after for the rest of their lives? You will have to make up your own answer for that. Will one or two of them have muscular dystrophy? Probably! Is it cruel to bring children into this world knowing they will be saddled with that horrible disability for their lifetime? They are the kind of questions that none of us can answer for anyone else because the answer is different for each of us. The reason, that we answer the way that we do, is part of how we are brought up, with a few genes thrown in.

I have a friend who said that my definition of a human being likened to a little red wagon with wheels. The wagon is filled with marbles replicated from the ones in our parents' wagon. When something went wrong, like muscular dystrophy, we could just take that marble out and replace it with another marble that did not have a defect. Now, this is a long way down the road but I believe it will eventually be true. I remember reading in someone's book about the body being a transportation system for genes. Think about that one for a while.

I wonder if I have talked to you about large schools. It seems like I remember saying something about it but I obviously had more to say because it is still on my mind. I know that anyone who came from the small high schools of the 50's and have had any contact with the big schools of the 90's know what I am talking about. Young people are not nourished by large schools. They are not made to feel that they are important. As a counselor, every student who came to see me was important and I honestly feel that I made a difference in his or her life. What about the ones who never found my office, the ones that were struggling academically, the ones who were not in the top classes or in the academic track. What about the ones who were not involved but who just watched, struggled and either dropped out, turned to alcohol or drugs and ended up being on 'the streets'. Most of these students did not have the self-confidence to walk into my office. It was the teacher who cared about them, who urged them to come. I am talking about that wonderful middle student, not the top, not the bottom, but the middle student.

I guess one of the people who made me think about this again was Richard and I know that I have not talked about him. He came from a family who had not made him a 'home'. You know, a place where he could feel safe, where the family ate together, played together, loved and encouraged each other. In such a family where school mattered, where it was the real father, mother, and neither of them drank or screamed at each other. That kind of home! A teacher referred him to me because he was thinking about dropping out.

That is another thing that I feel large schools cause, more dropouts. Isn't it ironic that just when, as a country, we focus on dropouts, we have large impersonal schools where students don't feel they belong? On with the story!

Richard said that his stepfather felt that he was wasting his time coming to school because he was barely passing his work, he wasn't involved in anything and he could be out making money instead of spending his stepfather's. He was out of a job more than he had one. Leave the education to people who care about it. He had never graduated from high school so he did not see why Richard felt that he should. I asked Richard if his stepfather drank. "Both of my parents drink all of the time. They are never there when I need them. They come home from work every day and start drinking. By dinnertime they are both drunk and start screaming at each other. The kids end up fixing what they eat. I am just sick and tired of it. I want to work and get my own place."

Now Richard was a senior and needed everything that he was taking to graduate. He was failing all of them and so badly that there was little hope of pulling them up. If I had ever talked to an at-risk student, he was one. He had four of the six major underlying factors that contribute to adolescents becoming at-risk students: alcoholism in the family, a stepfamily, lack of parental bonding, and poverty. One is too much but handling four is impossible. I was a little surprised that some of his teachers had not picked up on this before. I guessed that he was just a face in the classroom, never caused trouble, never raised his hand, never answered in class unless called on. He just sat there, absorbed in what? Absorbed in feelings of depression, failure and rejection, I am sure. I probably would have dropped out of school too if I had been him. I am sure that I would have felt a change in my life was bound to help. I felt the tears come in my eyes as he was talking. All I could do to help was to try to make him understand why he felt the way that he did. How he should think of the long-range effects of what he was doing rather than making a quick decision that would affect him the rest of his life. The bell rang and he promised to come back the next day and talk with me. I gave him a note to get out of class!

I sat there thinking about the statistics that I had read on alcoholism. Some of them are staggering. Did you know that if a student has one alcoholic parent, they have a 50% chance of becoming an alcoholic? If they have two alcoholic parents, they have an 80% chance. (National Council on Alcoholism, 1982). In a normal classroom of twenty-five students, four to six of those students have alcoholic parents (Morehouse and Scola 1986). The hair on the back of my neck stood up and a little chill passed over me. Should I let him go? I got up from my chair to call him back but decided against it because he had said that he had to go to work. I had a very positive feeling that I would be able to help this boy. We would be able to work something out for him.

He did come back the next day, thank goodness. He did listen to me when we talked about his options. He did think that giving up at this point in his life might be the wrong thing to do. We did not do what you might think! I ended up calling up the local community college to set up a meeting for him with them to talk about getting his GED (General Education Diploma). Now I am not pushing GED over high school education and I have never been sure, but I felt that it did make a difference with employers if you graduated from high school. I felt that they favored the student with a high school education. However, in his case I refused to saddle him with my middle class values. We had to do what was right for him in his depressed state. He promised that he would come back after he met with them and we would make some decisions, or a plan of action we called it.

He dropped out of school three days later, with my blessing, and entered the community college to get his GED. He sailed through that and his equivalency exam and received his diploma even before school was out. He opened a small vegetable stand the next year at a local shopping mall and at Christmas time, he carried Christmas trees. I bought one from him that year. He even came to my house and put it up. After Christmas, I got a thank you note from him for buying from him. I thought that I was the only one but it turned out that everyone who bought a tree got a thank you note. Now what do you think? How many times have you received a thank you note from someone who sold you a Christmas tree? He has a huge business now. He included plants, gifts, and vegetables and built a big building. He is very successful and it couldn't have happened to a nicer guy. Would he have done that if he had stayed in school that year? Would it have mattered if he had not received his GED? Who knows! However, I would like to think that being successful in school contributed to his success elsewhere and gave him the confidence to extend his horizons.

I guess that this is as good a place as any to talk about divorce. Alternatively, should I say children of divorce. I have never talked with children of divorced parents who were not having a hard time. Now remember that I am talking about high school students only. I don't know squat about elementary school children. I know that older children feel somehow that they are responsible for, or even the reason, that their parents divorce. They internalize this and carry it around with them for the rest of their lives. I have also never talked with one who did not fantasize about their parents getting back together.

Dick was one of these children. I guess that he represents all of them in my mind because when I heard him talk, I heard all of them. "It's my fault", he said. "I was the cause of the separation. I could just die. I am not sure what I did to cause it, but it was I. I feel so lost; you know it is like a death because he is not with me anymore. What is the difference in this and death? You know, it has robbed me of my lifestyle too. We do not have the money to do anything anymore. I guess that you would call us poor. It's always money, money, money. Most of all, it is just missing him being with us though. I am never going to get married! I had to leave all of my friends too. When Mother and I left we moved to an apartment, and I had to change schools. That's why I'm here. I am too old to have to make new friends though. I will be graduating this year and why even bother. I don't feel like talking with anyone anyway. I should have dropped out and just gone to work somewhere."

Every child that I have ever had any dealings with, who came from a divorced home says the same thing. It is a very rare case when the parents make a break that does not leave a scarred child. It is a vicious circle for children. First comes the divorce, then a great many at-risk behaviors occur such as early use of alcohol and drugs, poor school work, failure in classes and also dropping out of school. Hormones are raging anyway in high school students, this is just one more emotional thing for them to deal with, and it is out of their control.

I wondered, as I sat listening to him, if he had the stamina to work through some strategies to try to overcome his loss. He was about 5 foot ten and looked like he only weighed one hundred pounds. A strong wind would have blown him away. I really wondered if something else was also wrong with him. I mean, like medical problems. He had dark circles under his eyes and when he talked with me, he would not look at me. Just looking at him made me sad.

"Things just go around and around in my head," he said. "There is no beginning and no end and regardless of how hard I try, I can't make them stop. I feel that if I could ever get hold of them and find the end or the beginning, I could find a way out of this. Please help me before I go off the deep end. I can't stand this in my head anymore."

I had just started talking, searching for the right questions, when one of my guidance aids burst into my room. A deputy sheriff had come to tell me that a district court judge had subpoenaed my records on Wilma, one of my students!

Now, this was in the days before the state granted guidance counselor's privileged communication status and it was the first time that anyone had requested my records. Back in those dark ages, all of us kept records and notations from the sessions that we had with students. In addition, we wrote in the folders what actions we had taken, what we were going to do and some of the notes from what the students told us. I do not think that I did it because I was afraid that I would forget what I said. I think that it was more to remind me of what action I had taken when the student came back to see me. I also, sometimes wrote down what progress I thought that we had made. Many times, the student and I did it together so they could see the progress that they had made. It was very effective with some of them.

I did not know whether I should get up and refuse to give them to him or what. I did not know what the consequences were for not complying. In other words, I was stupid. I knew the deputy, he was one of my first students and he told me quick that I would go to jail if I refused. I ran through my mind what might be in the folder that would be detrimental to Wilma but I could not think of a thing. I did not know why they wanted it or what had happened to her.

I cannot remember the details. I do not know whether he took the record then or whether they made me bring it to court when I went. I was subpoenaed also. Anyway, some smart-ass lawyer had come up with the bright idea that subpoenaing her record would show how smart he was. He was making a grandstand play. It was a custody fight between her mother and father. She was living with her mother and the father wanted to prove that not only was she promiscuous but her mother allowed her to do anything that she wanted. Looking back on it, I think that my record pretty well attested to what he was trying to prove. She had come to see me first because she thought that she was pregnant. She was afraid to go to the doctor's office in town because she was afraid that she would see someone that she knew. She had heard that the health department would come out to the school and take blood for a pregnancy test if I called them and she wanted me to call. It turned out that she was not pregnant, but the fact that she was worried told you what she was doing.

Well, let me tell you, if you have never had a lawyer get you on the stand and twist your words around to what he wants to hear; you haven't lived. I do not know anything that is more degrading or more frustrating. I made a promise to myself when I was on that stand that I would never keep another record on a student as long as I lived and I never did.

I do not remember who she went to live with, but I am sure that the judge let her make the decision and I can only hope that it was the best one for her. I do remember wondering why the father wanted her to come and live with him so badly. He had never remarried and I think that I remembered that he had caught the mother running around on him. Was he trying to get back at the mother because of her infidelity, or was he interested in sex with his daughter. Sometimes you just think that way when you deal with it all the time.

It pains me to have to go back to Dick but I left you hanging and I need to finish up with him for you. He and I had fairly regular sessions for the next month. We worked through a lot of things that were bothering him. I found a beginning for him and we began the unraveling process and the count down. He missed one of our assigned meetings one day and I went looking for him. He was absent. When I called his house to find out where he was, someone there told me that he was in the hospital. He died a week later. Cancer, they said. I never hit on the right question!

CHAPTER 23

And Another Principal

I need to get on with this because I keep getting bogged down with individual cases and I know that you are getting weary. Anyway, I did not want to put this in because it is painful for me to remember but my next principal was a woman. Now I do not have anything against women. After all, I am one. However, if you have never had a woman boss you could never understand what I am explaining. I never asked for anything from her that I did not get, she never crossed me in any way. She let me do whatever I thought was best with no questions asked.

Not everybody who worked for her was that lucky. She was spiteful, vindictive, emotional, and manic-depressive. Is everybody in the public school system manic-depressive? She was on medication but on the right dosage though because most of the time she was under control.

She stayed in her office all of the time. She never walked the halls or saw a student unless they were in trouble. I think that her main job was to terrorize the teachers. In her meetings with them, if anything was said that she thought reflected badly on her, look out! She would call them down individually after the meeting and they had better change their attitude or she would personally see that they had nothing but grief from the office.

There was one wonderful teacher that she literally drove from the school; I mean she got him fired because he made a small off-handed statement in a teacher's meeting about the way that she handled parents. He stood behind his statement. He was right until the bitter end and the bitter end was that he was fired. The school suffered when he left so it was really our loss but she never saw it that way. She screamed; stuck things in his personnel folder that were not true, hounded him to death, even to the point of convincing the authorities that he was gay and not fit to teach kids. She could not have done that today but back then everybody agreed with that anyway, so she was on safe ground.

She attacked one of the men teachers when she found out he was dating one of the senior girls and fired him on the spot. She told him to go clean out his desk and never darken the school's doors again. That was what did her in. He was dating the student with the parent's approval and they went to bat for him. Two weeks later, he was reinstated and she had to issue a public apology to him. What a mess.

She would always have these little séances with the assistance principal, she was a woman also, and you could see them with their heads together whispering and gossiping and plotting. God forbid that I would ever have to be a part of that huddle. She lacked compassion and when you are dealing with children, you need a lot of compassion. All the teachers tiptoed around, afraid to make a sound. No one spoke up for anything that the principal had not said that she was for first. That is no way to run a school. I have told you before that the students reflect the attitude of the teachers. They were afraid also. Half of them did not know what she looked like because she never came out of that office. I wonder if she was afraid of the students'.

CHAPTER 24

The Unswept Corners

It was about this time that I met Renee. Renee lived in that gray zone. The blacks hated her because she worked hard, made good grades, and studied. The whites would not have anything to do with her because she was black. Therefore, she was a loner, a sad loner. Young people can be so cruel, honest and cruel. To me she was beautiful, intelligent and witty. Her father had been an educator, a pillar in the black community before integration, a nothing after integration and had died of a heart attack soon after things settled down. Her mother had never worked and was almost a recluse. Renee was an only child and came to see me because she was torn between attending a black university or a predominately-white university. Her mother wanted her to go to a black school and her grandmother wanted her to attend a white school. It is a wonder that I had not been tarred, feathered and run out of town on a rail by this time because, as I am sure that you realize from reading this far, I used directive counseling on quite a few occasions. In fact, I used it more times than I would like to admit.

I told her right off the bat that I felt she would have a great many more job opportunities if she attended a white prestigious university. We all know that it is not what you learn in college or what you majored in when you go to get a job. It is whom you or your parents know or knew. Don't get on your high horse; think about it. Think of all of the people that you know and how they got their jobs. Black kids had a hard time in a white world because they didn't have any contacts. Even with contacts, the contacts did not back them.

I knew that her mother would end up hating me but maybe the grandmother could explain it all to her. The black colleges would hate me if they knew it but facts are facts. She ended up telling me about all of her frustrations on that very first visit. Perhaps the directness started her off, who knows. She told me about never having anyone to eat with, no one to go to the movies with, no one to ever gossip with, and worst of all, no one to even study with in a study group. There were no friends!

In our subsequent meetings, she was open to the point of embarrassment on some issues. She seemed to fail to realize that I was wearing the counselor hat and not the friend hat. I could see that I was going to have trouble easing her out of counseling because she was becoming dependent on the relationship. Hell, I do not blame her. I would feel the same way too. I began to plot and plan about a boyfriend for her. What is the old adage? You can lead a horse to water but you can't make him drink. In this case, can't make her drink.

I suggested that maybe she could write me notes when she thought about something that she would like to tell me rather than come down out of class. She rejected this at first but then she started writing to me and she would leave the notes under my door before she left school. They were beautiful notes and I saved them all and made a little scrap book out of them for her. I thought that one day I would return them to her when she was more comfortable with her world. I only hoped that one day she would be.

She enrolled at Harvard in the fall and I saw her two or three times during that time but it was after she finished law school that she came to see me and I gave her the notes. At that time, she was a promising young lawyer with a very prestigious law firm somewhere. She said that the hardest thing that she had to learn was that what she thought mattered. I have told you that before in this book. It seems to be a recurring theme among intelligent blacks from the South. Remember that when you deal with them. She loved the notes and said that she would cherish them forever and she hugged my neck. She said that had it not been for me she would have never made it. Now we all know that's a bunch of hooey but it was so nice for her to say it. That kind of talk will keep you going for another two or three years. People in education very rarely receive praise for good deeds. Remember that.

It is a wonder that people in the ivory towers cannot see why 40% of the students who drop out, drop out. It really is very simple. They have to work to make money to have a car to drive to work. Does that make sense? Wheels they call it. All of the new high schools are out in the country and everybody who is anybody has a car. God forbid if a high school student has to ride a bus. They are a nobody. Our state rule is that if you live more than a mile from the school that you attend, the school system has to provide transportation for you, hence the buses. Almost everyone lives more than a mile from his or her high school. Students may not drive the buses; they must be driven by adults. This is all a lead into Jimmy.

Now Jimmy was not a bad student. I cannot say that he did any studying but he was passing everything. He was in sort of a general curriculum but college was not for him. He kept missing school. You know that if you miss too many days the teachers must automatically fail you with a 69. This is regardless of whether or not you are passing. Crazy isn't it. If that teacher is doing anything in class, if seems to me that you would have to be there to pass. If you were not there, you would miss all that she is doing. I keep going around in circles, but it is confusing. Anyway, Jimmy was passing but not there enough days to pass. That's as good as I can do with this. Therefore, he ended up in my office.

"Wheels", he said. "I have to have wheels. I sure as hell am not going to ride that bus. If I did not work, I would not be able to date, much less come to school. How can you date without a car?" My vocabulary has deteriorated exponentially with the number of years that I worked with young people. I spent my whole young adult life without using a four-letter word but from then on, it has been all down hill. If there is one that I have not used I would be surprised. My middle class friends raise their eyebrows at me sometimes.

"Nobody is questioned you working", I said, "only the fact that you are missing school so much."

"Well lady, I guess that it all boils down to the fact that having a car is more important to me than having an education. If it is a choice between the two, a car wins every time. They call me in to work, I go. I have to keep that job because I am barely making enough to buy gas now."

"Why are you coming to school at all," I asked, "If you are failing everything then you are wasting your time here. Quit and get you a full time job and spend the rest of your life cooking hamburgers." Well, it just slipped out; I could not help it. I never should have said it and I knew it, but there it was lying on the table. He looked at me kind of sideways. You know with your head tilted over.

"You're right, I'll quit today," and he walked out! I felt worse that day than almost any day of my counseling life and I wanted to lie down and cry or get in my Mother's lap or something like that. I did not go after him. I knew that it would do no good. I knew instinctively that the lines of communication had been broken and he was gone.

As to end of the story, I am not sure that there is an end, or that there ever will be. However, he did come back the next year and he did graduate. He never came into my office that whole year. He did very well, made good grades and even took some college preparatory courses.

At graduation, as the line was marching out to the field, he passed me and said very simply, "Thank you". That was the end of that.

CHAPTER 25

Retirement

Yes, there does come a time for retirement. That occurred for me ten years ago. I left that counseling world and the wonderful students.

I need to tell you here that if you have never read *Raising Children In A Socially Toxic Environment* by James Garbarino, you should read it. He probably understands where young people are coming from far better than any author that I have ever read. His thoughts on TV for young people, what parents are all about, poverty, and what it does to young people, how some of them make it out of the muck, all of that stuff. He hits the nail on the head. If you have ever had children, or work with young people, or care about them, read that book. However, on with my story.

I felt that I needed to tie up a few things before I left you. I was recently at a presentation of awards for achievement at a local college. The front two rows were filled with the recipients and I kept hearing the man about four people down from me talking before the program started. There was something about the voice that struck a chord in my memory. The man was very nice-looking, gray hair like me and he had on a purple coat. He was talking in a very loud voice and I asked one of the men siting next to me who he was.

"Why that's Raz Autry," he said. I almost fell out of my seat. Here I was siting on the same row with the marine principal who had started me on my career as a counselor and I didn't even recognize him! Both of us were getting awards on the same day. I got up and walked over and stood right in front of him.

"Hello Raz," I said. I could tell by the look in his eyes that he was searching for a name to put with the face. Isn't it interesting that people who meant so much to each other at a different time in their lives forget. The memory of the person is still there but the face looks so different from what you remember.

I immediately said, "I was your first guidance counselor," and said my name. He grabbed me in a bear hug and hooped and hollered all around. We talked and talked about so many things until the program started and both promised to meet afterwards. Afterwards, the families and the well-wishers crowded around and we unfortunately never saw each other again.

Gerald Maynor? Yes, I looked up Gerald many, many years after my times with him. He had become the Dean of Students at Pembroke State University, his alma mater. They told me he had died of a massive heart attack early in life and they had dedicated a building to him. How wonderful! He will always be remembered there. The dedication plaque told all about who he was and how much all of the students had loved him. It told how he had left a vacancy on the faculty that would never be filled. It seemed that his family had helped to build the building that bore his name. I guessed that they meant the family had given the money.

I also saw another of my principals. It was in a nursing home in an Alzheimer's unit. He did not even know who I was. I had worked with him for over 25 years. Life can be so cruel sometimes. A couple of the counselors who worked with me have since died, a few of cancer, a few of just old age, but some are still working like me. They are still trying to make a difference.

I realize that this book reeks with darkness and shadows. It is filled with abuse, incest, dire poverty, the oppression of religious fanaticism on children. It includes uncaring parents, defeated parents, drugged parents, and all other specters imaginable. I have brought darkness into your life. Forgive me. It is very hard to remember the bright sun-shiny things that happen, but somehow you do not forget the hardships and the sadness that you see. People who see the bright side of everything are not the kind of people that counselors usually see. Have you figured out that most of the shadows come from the home? Should we sterilize everyone who is poor or mentally deficient? What nonsense!

There are some avenues that I think the public school systems should pursue. One of the main ones is to get the parents into the school, or go to where the parents are. Somehow, try to reach them. I know this may sound silly but the federal government spends zillions of dollars on all these programs for dropout prevention and the 'No Child Left Behind' programs and the 'what have you' programs. Why not feed the parents of the children who are on free and reduced lunch. I mean, give a free meal to the parents. Let them ride the bus in if you have to, for lunch, dinner, breakfast, any time. Go get them, let them have one good meal a day. Think of all the things that you could do while you had them captive.

We could change the curriculum from a group-oriented way of thinking about young people to one that addresses the interests, inclinations, and talents of the individual student. I am not talking just about high school; I am talking about the whole school system. I do not think that there is a scientifically confirmed theory of learning supporting the school curriculum. Not only that, I think we fail children because they are not meeting the expectations of the 'experts' as Bruce Goldberg says in *Why Schools Fail* (Cato Institute), but rather because the 'experts' are failing because they are not meeting the children where they are. I think that a lot of wonderful teachers have learned how to individualize their class-room to meet the needs of all kinds of students. They have had to, but how hard it is, even for them, to keep the best and the brightest way up there where they should be. This is especially true when they have twenty students or more with no aid.

High school becomes more selective because students choose the courses they want but you know what happens. They don't choose the hard courses because they don't want to work. They will always take the easy way out if someone does not push them. Parents who don't care don't push. These parents do not have education as a priority. The job is what they think is important, any job, and they want the kid out working and making money. Consequently, their students get the short end of the stick. They never are challenged. They never catch up. They start off behind; they end up behind. Behind is forever for them.

We can only hope that they will find some caring person who will help them along the way. It may not be a parent but just some other reference person that the student can trust and respect. These types of relationships can teach the student to trust, respond, and help to build self-confidence. That is us!!

I see my students running the world now. Everywhere I go, they are there. I see a nurse in the hospital, a fitness expert in the gym, a waitress, a doctor, a janitor, a secretary, a housewife, a lawyer. How wonderful it was to have shared some of their life with them. When I see some of them, I know that I made a difference in their life and I smile because I know that they made it. They might not have made it in my definition of the word, but they made it in their definition and that is what's important

When I think back over my counseling career, I do not think that I would have changed one thing about any of it. I thank young people whose path crossed mine for letting me share their life with them and for making my life richer for having done so.

CHAPTER 26

Operating a Scholarship Program

You thought that those words above were the end, didn't you? Well, I did too but the more I thought about an end, the more I realized I could not leave you thinking that this book was some outdated nonsense that had no relevance in today's world. Therefore, I must go on. I must carry you to the end.

Although my counseling work stopped, my work did not. There was just something about being involved that was important to me. I had the opportunity to help set up a really wonderful scholarship program for young people. This was one that encompassed every aspect that I felt young people needed to make a success out of their high-school years. The program was really different. The student was held responsible for things like attendance, discipline, involvement in community service, grades, and they were even required to remain drug-free (the kids laughed at this but the majority were honest about their involvement). In return, they were provided with mentors, peer counseling, parents involvement with their school and with their teachers. To top it all off, they received a $1500 scholarship for each year that they met all of their requirements. At the end of four years of high school, there it was, a four-year college education at a state supported school! Neat!

One of the things that I really loved about the program was that the parents were required to meet with the students' teachers once every six weeks. Now talk about getting the parents in the school, this was amazing. All kind of great things came from this.

The *Life Long Learning* (L3) program was created in 1992 and it was set up just to serve the students of our county It was a very innovative program to provide students access to post-secondary education and to raise student and community expectations regarding *Life Long Learning.* It is an exclusive program that depends on private donations to guarantee students the opportunity for higher education and a chance for a better and more rewarding future. All students in the school system were eligible regardless of family income or financial circumstances. Students, parents, business leaders, mentors, and the entire county community were included as a part of the concept, each group contributing to the overall success. I authored a book that describes the program in detail and results. It is called *Life Long Learning,* July 1, 1999 and is available from me.

As you see throughout this book, the need for student help in this county was very high.

Pardon me while I cite a few statistics. High school graduation in the county was 36% and ranked 37th out of 100 counties. The county ranked well below the national average in percentage of college graduates. Per capita spending was below the state average. Post-secondary education was stagnant for high school graduates and well below the state average.

Growth was occurring all around us and opportunities were opening up for students with education, but this growth helped little for undereducated youngsters living in trailers.

County students face increasingly fierce competition. The county growth is in knowledge industries such as pharmaceuticals, computers and software. These require higher level workers and reject the county residents that are not prepared to participate.

L3 was designed to incorporate the community in each student's lonely and perilous climb toward education, employment and citizenship. Students often lack family inspiration, positive family social values, supportive attitudes and money. Poverty and race were also crucial factors. To many, their plight seemed hopeless and students settled often for a fate far less than promised by their potential. All these factors were addressed by L3.

The L3 program required a formal contract with the participating students as they progress from class to class. If the contract is fulfilled, they are given financial assistance to pursue their education through college or in a formal life-long learning process. The contract called for performance against state criteria in several areas including academics, attendance, citizenship, drug and alcohol abstinence and parental involvement in critical school activities. L3 also addressed family pursuit of scholarships and assistance funding outside L3 and student community service. All these are critical for student's success. Successful high school students were given a share each year. There was immediate ownership to be used after graduation. In August 1995, it was feared that the program was financially overexposed and could not be further financed, a fear that later proved exaggerated.

All the members of the school board agreed L3 was so appealing because it made no distinctions in class, race, or culture. It was not limited to low-income students, the wealthy, or the middle class; but it encompassed those of all income levels, avoiding any stigma.

All of the data collected evidenced that the program was a phenomenal success. Over 4,000 people in this small community were involved in the program, all striving for one goal. That goal was to help young people succeed. The most tremendous success may have occurred in areas that could not be measured, such as students' parents pride in their school, parental involvement in every phase of high school life, students' excitement about the opportunities that would be open to them and the encouragement that the students received from the community. The list could go be a long one.

Everyone in the community was involved. Everyone was excited and the excitement carried over to the students. One of the beauties of the concept was rather than something being given to the student for free, the student had to work for the guarantee. The guarantee was for a better life through education. They were assured that if they met their responsibilities, they would be given a path to work in a more meaningful job. Thereby, the life and experiences they and their families could enjoy would be significantly enriched.

The L3 program focused on the performance of students. It required greater participation by parents in school affairs, closer supervision of student progress by school administrators, and a deeper commitment from the community and its leaders in uplifting the quality of our schools. The important milestones for the program were definitive, measurable and resulted from the participation of school leaders, students, parents, community and contributors.

Reinforcing the poor economics of the county are the following statistics. The Median Household Income for the county was $12,320 in 1980, $30,269 in 1990 and $54,089 in 2009. The Per Capita Personal Income was $5,331 in 1980, $14,854 in 1990 and $23,399 in 2009. Clearly, this is a struggling county that is unprepared for the present, much less for the future.

Funding rested with the County Education Foundation. After 3 years operation of L3, there was fear that the funding would become exhausted. It was decided to stop the program. The funding was taken out of the L3 program and given to the Foundation. After a few years, it became obvious that the exposure was less than had been predicted. A different program was instituted whereby a single scholarship is given to one person from each high school in the county. This program continues.

In spite of the need, the huge undertaking and the obvious ringing success, the program melted mostly away. That is too bad.

The program was fantastic. The young people were fantastic too. The money was not! We raised a million dollars but that was far short of the three million dollars that we needed to perpetuate the program. Therefore, the program shut down. We spent the next nine years paying out the scholarship shares to students who had earned them during the four years that the program operated for all of the high schools in the county including the same school where I had counseled.

One of my favorite stories during this time was about a tall handsome black boy who wanted to attend truck driver's training school. He had only earned one scholarship share of $1500 but this was plenty to get him through that program. Now visualize a kid with no car, no phone, no bank account, no way to cash a check, on welfare, thinking he could learn to drive an eighteen-wheeler. Talk about reaching for a star!

He showed up in my office one day and I took him to the admissions office of a local truck driver's training school and paid his tuition. He took the little test and failed. He failed the drug test too. That's when he told me he was on probation for drug possession and he didn't even have a driver's license! Damn!

You can imagine how he and I spent the next year and his $1500.

I went to his graduation a year later and saw him drive off in his eighteen-wheeler with everybody who was ever kin to him looking on. There must have been thirty people there. He's on the road now with you somewhere helping to make the world go round.

CHAPTER 27

Return to Duty

Don't get impatient. I am getting to the last chapter of this book. You will never guess what happened then! Since you cannot guess, I'll tell you. I went back to my old school, part time, mind you. I could tell you that I could not stand not working or I could tell you that they begged me to come back. I missed the kids. That is the long and short of it!

I thought that returning would be easy but it was the hardest thing that I have ever done. Well, at least the second hardest. The first was when I was talked into teaching Honors Biology to a high school class when I had not been in a Biology class for 40 years. That was harder than having a baby.

All of the old images and feelings flooded into my mind when I walked into that guidance department. There hung my picture on the wall; there was my same office where I sat for thirty years and talked to all of those wonderful students. It was not mine this time; another counselor occupied it. It took me a while to catch my breath and dig in.

Things had not changed. There were still over two hundred students waiting to enroll or change schedules. There were still ninety teachers overloaded in their classrooms; some had as many as forty kids in a class with twenty-eight chairs. What a mess the start of a new school year brings.

I really thought that I was too old to relate to young people, too many wrinkles, you know. There was that kind of thing but it didn't seem to matter to the students. They talked as they always did. They looked me right in the eye and the words flowed out.

Oh, I forgot to tell you. This school was now 45% black, 15% Mexican, and 40% white.

As I said, there has been a tremendous increase in the Mexican population in this rural county in the last ten years, mostly what used to be migrant farm workers. Now, they stay year-round.

One of the first boys that I talked with was black. His uncle had brought him in and as they sat down across the table from me, I said, "I know your father." The boy was a dead ringer for a previous student of mine. There was the most surprised look on his face when I called his father's name. "You look just like him. He was one of my students a long time ago." I thought the uncle was going to fall out of his chair, and out it came.

"I thought we all looked alike to white people." Nothing had changed, still the same old feelings. Actually, the boy that I was thinking of was this student's grandfather. We fixed his schedule just like he wanted it

The uncle said to me, "If he gives you any trouble, call me." In addition, he handed me his phone number. Now isn't that something? A school with 1500 students and the uncle thinks I would know if the boy acts up.

I sometimes think that computers were invented by the devil. People old like me want to write everything out in long hand because that is the way that they learned to do it and that is the way that they think. Then they have to type it all out to spell the words right and they takes forever.

Anyway, I wanted to tell you about my trip to Washington on the train. We have a small train stop in a town about four miles from where I live but you have to reserve a ticket. You call ahead. They reserve a ticket on the phone and you pay the conductor when you get on the train. A little man comes out, puts down the steps and puts your luggage on for you. I guess this is pretty standard procedure. After he got me all settled he took me to the conductor for me to buy my ticket. A very handsome Indian man sat at the table in a conductor's uniform. He said, "I know you don't remember me, Mrs. Jones. I was one of your students many years ago in high school," and he named the school. I did not recognize him; after all, it had been almost 40 years. Where did all of those years go? It seemed like yesterday when I was there. He continued, "If it had not been for you, I probably would still be sleeping on my dirt floor but you made me feel like I was somebody and I owed it to myself to BE somebody. I went to Pembroke University and I never looked back. Thank you."

I figured that I might get to learn something about my old counseling buddy, Gerald Maynor, the big Indian counselor that I told you about many chapters ago. I said, "Tell me if you know anything about Gerald Maynor. I have not heard from him in years." He looked at me sorta funny and said, 'Don't you remember Mrs. Jones? He was my Grandfather. He died of a heart attack a few years back." I was treated royally on that train trip into Washington.

I can hardly go anywhere in Eastern North Carolina without someone recognizing me and saying wonderful things to me about how I helped them when they were in school, but I did so little. I only listened.

The reason that I wanted to tell you about this was that I wanted to be sure that I made the point again about how little it takes to make a difference in someone's life and how special you feel when they tell you about it. Living in my community is the same way. I have a special place in so many people's lives and from the very richest to the very poorest. I am reminded almost every day that I made a difference. It seemed like a very small difference to me but to children with fragile wings it seemed monumental.

My first class graduated in 1974 is almost 60 years old now and that is a lot of grandfathers, fathers, and children whose paths I crossed. Almost everyone in my social group had children who now have children, and who now have children. All of these are part of my background.

All of the Mexicans that I encountered when I came back were a surprise to me. When I left this school ten years ago, there was one Mexican enrolled in the 12th grade. Her name was Gloria. She had entered our school as a ninth grader and she did not speak a word of English. They called me down to the office to try to help them extract the information from her. You know how people do when they are talking to someone who speaks a foreign language. They talk louder and louder because somehow they feel if they talk loud enough, the person will finally understand them. That was where they were when I walked in. It was a screaming match.

It turned out that the French teacher spoke a little Spanish and I mean a little. We put Gloria in French for two periods and in math. That's kinda like a universal language and left her to 'fish or cut bait', so to speak. She didn't even get one of our textbooks in Spanish. We tried but we never could find one.

Gloria would leave school at the end of April and enroll in a school in Florida. She would come back in November because her family was migrant farm workers and they followed the growing season. She would come back in November and re-enroll in our school. Each time we would jiggle all the grades around to make them match our courses and so it went this way for four years. That last year she did not leave in April. She stayed until the first week in June and graduated 8th in her class of 365. So much for the language barrier! She was driven to graduate from high school in the States and that is what she did. I never saw her again after that night but I know wherever she is and whatever she is doing, she is successful.

They now have Spanish teachers in the high school; we have two. They teach no one but students who have English as a second language. The students can graduate out of this program into regular classrooms once they master English.

I registered many of these kids that first two weeks of school. The family brought the students to school. When I say family, I mean family: mother, daddy, sisters, brothers, uncles, aunts, and babies. They all came as a group. We were even hard pushed to find enough chairs for them all to sit in. They didn't interrupt or comment and it was usually the student we were enrolling who spoke the best English, but everyone was there supporting them.

All of the students without exception wanted to know what I thought they should do, what class did I think they belonged in, what lunch should they have. There was a softness about them that I had not found in other students, a shyness almost. Even the boys had this look in their eyes. I think that I will be honored to be able to get to know them better. I might even get over being ticked off at all of those announcements in Spanish at Wal-Mart.

The thought came to me that I never talked to any students about homosexuality. I am sure that topic would come up today. Times are different in that arena

I never talked with any girls or boys back then who tried normal sex and did not like it. I do remember that even I did not know what a homosexual was until I was in college. Maybe they were in the same boat. I am sure that all of the experimenting with your emotions must come first. I did talk with a lot of students that I was suspicious of, especially black males for some reason. But, who knows?

I went to a statewide counselors meeting and during coffee, I was introduced to one of the admissions directors from UNC Chapel Hill. I knew immediately that he was a Lumbee Indian; those beautiful green eyes looked at me out of that brown face.

"Did you happen to know a man named Gerald Maynor?" I asked.

"He was my father-in-law," the man said. What a small world we live in. I told him all about my wonderful experiences with Gerald, my BIG Indian mentor counselor, and how we started out together so many years ago. He loved it!

The students have not changed. They still have the same problems, the same attitudes. They are still pregnant and some do not know how they got that way. When school had been open for only two weeks, there had already been two fights in the lunch room. Who was fighting? You know, it came from their neighborhoods and they brought it to school with them, just like in the old days.

I haven't seen any "baggy pants". They have a dress code now but I bet when they get off the school grounds those pants come down.

My new principal? He's tall, handsome, and young, and he wears black shirts and black pants and purple ties. He has great plans to get the school back on track and make it a flagship school for the state. Perhaps he can, who knows!

I hope that the school and the students will flourish with him and everyone will grow strong wings.

CHAPTER 28

And Yet Another School

I was called to fill in for another counselor who had a nervous breakdown. I would not have taken this job but the principal was a student of mine and he was so pitiful that it would have broken my heart to say no. He came by the house and got down on his knees begging me to help him (not really). How could I say no! I told him that I would help him out if he would continue looking to hire someone else and if my job was only for a short time.

No doubt this will be my last counseling experience (but who knows). It is at a school where all of the so-called "bad boys" were sent from every high school in the county. For those of you who are not in the "know" this was called an alternative school. The students who attended here could not fit into a regular structured school environment. They were sent for different lengths of time depending on the infraction. It could have been for drug use, for carrying a gun to school, for hitting a teacher, for fighting, for acting out in class, for any of a long list of infractions, real or imagined.

I could understand why the counselor had a nervous breakdown after I had been there one day.

It was one of the most rewarding times of my counseling career. I bet there was not one student at this school who had two parents at home. Half of them did not have one parent at home. There were uncles, brothers, girlfriends, grandparents, Social Services, wards of the court, foster parents and friends at the place they went home to from school. Some of them came to school from the jail and went back to the jail after school. After all, they had free lunch and a bus ride to and from school. There was no way they could miss those two treats in their bleak life. Clothes, they had no clothes, some of them wore the same shirt the whole time that I was there and I know that it was never washed.

A few of them had really bad attitudes but the majority was sweet caring boys and girls who so badly needed someone to care about them. Naturally, I worked until the end of the year and we graduated four of them. This was the school's first graduating class! Only two of them had enough money to buy caps and gowns for graduation. The faculty pitched in and bought them for the other two. Three of them did not have any way to get to the school because the buses had stopped running and faculty members had to go and pick them up. They were so proud and so happy that I had to cry through the whole ceremony.

Each one of them made a little speech when they walked across to get their diploma and every one of them told little stories about how much the school had meant to them and how happy they were. For what? No car, no money, nobody to help them, no way to climb out of the hole they were born in, no way to work or get to work. No way to get off the porch.

Both of the schools that I talk about are what I consider average for 'large' high schools today, both in size and general population, anywhere in the U.S. It does not matter whether they are urban, rural, and rich or poor. The problems are the same. Again, I want to make it clear to the reader the students that I talk about represent less than 2% of the population in both of the school's. The majority of the students have wonderful parents; they are well adjusted, bright and motivated to make wise decisions. These students have problems too, serious problems, and some of them are addressed here. However, the 2% that I deal with most have nowhere else to turn and need help to learn to fly.

I have had many awards pass my way over the years. My picture hangs in the Educators Hall of Fame at East Carolina University. I was selected by the Federal Government to explain the Financial Aid Applications for the state of North Carolina to all of the counselors in the state as part of the Pell Grant program. However, my most prized award was the Living Legend Award presented to me by our County School System. The inscription on this award says: "To a person who retired from our ranks who, while with us and continuing today, cares more than others think is wise, risks more than others think is safe, dreams more than others think is practical, expects more than others think is possible, succeeds far more than peers can imagine, and gives freely from the heart everyday of her life in the service of others".

Isn't that pretty?

The End

www.ingramcontent.com/pod-product-compliance
Lightning Source LLC
Chambersburg PA
CBHW021541260326
41914CB00001B/111
* 9 7 8 1 6 0 4 1 4 5 5 4 0 *